COMPENSATION
AND
REHABILITATION

TO MY PARENTS

COMPENSATION
AND
REHABILITATION

A Survey of the Report of the National Committee of Inquiry
into Compensation and Rehabilitation in Australia and the
National Compensation Bill 1974.

by

HAROLD LUNTZ BA, LLB (Witwatersrand), BCL (Oxon)
Reader in Law, University of Melbourne
Barrister and Solicitor of the Supreme Court of Victoria

BUTTERWORTHS

Sydney   **Melbourne**   Brisbane

1975

AUSTRALIA:

BUTTERWORTHS PTY LTD
586 Pacific Highway, Chatswood 2067
343 Little Collins Street, Melbourne 3000
Commonwealth Bank Building, King George Square, Brisbane 4000
49-51 St Georges Terrace, Perth 6000

NEW ZEALAND:

BUTTERWORTHS OF NEW ZEALAND LTD
New Zealand Law Society Building,
26-28 Waring Taylor Street, Wellington 1

ENGLAND:

BUTTERWORTH & CO (PUBLISHERS) LTD
88 Kingsway, London, WC2B 6AB

CANADA:

BUTTERWORTH & CO (CANADA) LTD
14 Curity Avenue, Toronto 374, Ontario

SOUTH AFRICA:

BUTTERWORTH & CO (SA) (PTY) LTD
152-154 Gale Street, Durban

National Library of Australia
Cataloguing-in-Publication entry

Luntz, Harold
 Compensation and rehabilitation: a
survey of the report of the National
Committee of Inquiry into Compensation and
Rehabilitation in Australia and the National
compensation bill 1974/by Harold Luntz.—
Sydney: Butterworths, 1975.
Index.
ISBN 0 409 37886 0.
1. Australia. Law, statutes, etc. Bills.
Bill for a National Compensation Act 1974.
2. Compensation (Law) — Australia.
3. Rehabilitation — Australia — Law and
legislation. I. Title.
344.9402

Printed in Australia by
Simmons Limited, Sydney
for the publishers Butterworths Pty Ltd

CONTENTS

PREFACE

This book is written on the assumption that the National Compensation Bill 1974 will be passed by the Australian Parliament and come into operation on 1st July 1976. That assumption may prove to be false. At the present time the Bill is under consideration by the Senate Committee on Constitutional and Legal Affairs. The Bill and the <u>Report of the National Committee of Inquiry into Compensation and Rehabilitation in Australia</u> 1974 ("the Woodhouse Report"), which spawned it, are the subject of some public debate. Owing to the necessary technicality of many of the provisions of the Bill, there has perhaps been less understanding of the proposals than of any other major piece of social reform of recent years. As with other recent legislative innovations, much of the public discussion has been misinformed as to the true consequences of the proposed changes. It is hoped that this book will contribute to a proper understanding of the proposed National Compensation Scheme and will enable debate on its merits to proceed without misrepresentation.

It will be clear to any reader that I myself am strongly in favour of the principles on which the Bill is based and am in accord with most of its detailed provisions. The criticisms that I have made of some clauses are offered in the hope that amendments will lead to the removal of flaws in the total fabric of the scheme. If my criticism is not always constructive, other, more original, minds may be stimulated to finding solutions for seemingly intractable problems.

If the Bill does become law substantially in its present form, the commentary here offered will, I hope, be useful as a guide to the interpretation of an Act which, while a model of succinctness, will not always be easy to follow. The success of the National Compensation Scheme will largely depend on those called upon to administer it. To them, and to all who may wish to know the rights of the injured and sick under the scheme, I hope this book will provide assistance.

Thanks are due to Richard Thomas, for reading the whole manuscript, and to Gary Evans and Greg Terry, for assuring me that I have said nothing outrageously inaccurate in the section on Constitutional Validity. The views expressed throughout are, of course, my own. Joan Naylor and her team of typistes at the Melbourne Law School were responsible for producing a typed form of my manuscript that was as free of typing errors as humanly possible. The final version, which the reader can here see reproduced and the high quality of which he can thus judge for himself, was typed by Jean Turner. Finally, I must record the sacrifice which my family made of much of the Christmas-New Year holiday period so that the work could be completed in accordance with my undertaking to the publishers.

H L

February 1975

TABLE OF SECTIONS

NATIONAL COMPENSATION BILL 1974 (cont)

Chapter 1

HISTORY AND PHILOSOPHY

Sec 1: THE COMMITTEE OF INQUIRY

1.101 Early in 1973, having been in office only a matter of weeks, the Australian Labor Government established a committee to consider the scope, form and administration of a national rehabilitation and compensation scheme. It appointed a committee comprising Sir Owen Woodhouse, as chairman, Mr Justice C L D Meares and Professor P S Atiyah.

1.102 Mr Justice Woodhouse. Sir Owen Woodhouse, a judge of the Court of Appeal in New Zealand, had previously headed an inquiry into that country's workers' compensation legislation. In a revolutionary report,[1] published in 1967, the New Zealand Woodhouse Committee had proposed the replacement of common law actions for damages for personal injury, as well as workers' compensation, by a comprehensive scheme of compensation. That report was subject to detailed scrutiny in a New Zealand Government White Paper,[2] which was mainly concerned with the costing of the scheme, and by a select committee of both parties in

1. Report of the Royal Commission of Inquiry into Compensation for Personal Injury in New Zealand, 1967.
2. Personal Injury: A Commentary on the Report of the Royal Commission of Inquiry into Compensation for Personal Injury in New Zealand, 1969.

the New Zealand Parliament.[3] Late in 1972 the New
Zealand legislature enacted a long, complex statute to
give effect to the major recommendations of the report.
That Act was in turn much amended before it came into
operation on 1st April 1974.[4] It should be stressed at
this stage that the Australian proposals which are
discussed hereafter, though based on similar principles
to those contained in the original New Zealand report,
differ considerably from the scheme which finally
emerged in New Zealand.

1.103 <u>Other Members</u>. Mr Justice Meares is a judge
of the Supreme Court of New South Wales, who has had
considerable experience in personal injury litigation.
He is also chairman of the New South Wales Law Reform
Commission and of the Expert Group on Road Safety,
which in 1972 presented a report to the then Minister
for Shipping and Transport on road accidents in
Australia. Professor Atiyah was at the time of his
appointment a professor of law at the Australian
National University. He has written extensively on the
Law of Torts and in 1970 published a book entitled
<u>Accidents, Compensation and the Law</u>, which is concerned
with evaluating the policies which underlie the different systems operating for the compensation of people
injured in the United Kingdom. For personal reasons
Professor Atiyah had to return to England before the
work of the committee was completed. Though he is not
a signatory of the report, it seems that he endorses at
least its major conclusions.[5]

3. <u>Report of the Select Committee on Compensation for
    Personal Injury</u>, 1970.
4. For a summary of the New Zealand legislation see
    D R Harris, "Accident Compensation in New Zealand:
    A Comprehensive Insurance System" (1974) 37 Mod L
    Rev 361. Earlier articles on the scheme are
    listed <u>ibid</u>, nn 3-5.
5. See his letter to the London <u>Times</u>, 7/12/74.

1.104   Assistants. The committee had the assistance of Professor G W R Palmer of the Faculty of Law of the Victoria University of Wellington, who had done much work in connexion with the New Zealand scheme, and of a team of statisticians and legal researchers, as well as administrative staff. Mr J Q Evans, CMG, CBE, until his recent retirement First Parliamentary Counsel to the Australian Government, drafted a Bill which was attached to the report to explain some of the more detailed aspects of the recommendations and to provide a basis for legislation if the recommendations of the committee proved acceptable to the Government. Compared to the prolixity of the New Zealand Act the Bill is a model of conciseness.

1.105   Gathering Evidence. The terms of reference of the committee (see Sec 2) were widely advertised and written submissions from interested organizations and persons were invited. Subsequently, public hearings were held in the capital cities of all the States of Australia. Background papers were also circulated with invitations to comment on specific issues. Mr Justice Meares and members of the statistical team made investigations in a number of countries overseas.

1.106   Report. At the end of June 1974, after some fifteen months of inquiry, the committee presented its report to the Prime Minister. Volume 1, dealing with the compensation proposals in detail and matters of rehabilitation and safety in summary form, and also containing a draft National Compensation Bill, was published in printed form in July 1974. Volume 2, which elaborates the recommendations with regard to rehabilitation and safety, followed shortly thereafter. A third volume, called "The Compendium", was issued in duplicated form in September. This volume contains copies of the public advertisements; background papers;

statistical information relating to the incidence of
injury and sickness, the cost of present compulsory
third party insurance and workers' compensation schemes
and estimates of the cost of the committee's proposed
scheme; a comparison of the benefits under the proposed
scheme with awards of damages at common law in a series
of cases in the Supreme Court of New South Wales; and
certain correspondence with the representatives of the
legal profession in Victoria.

Sec 2:   TERMS OF REFERENCE OF THE COMMITTEE

1.201 **Injury.** When the committee was established it
was given the following terms of reference:

> To inquire into and report on the scope and form
> of, and the manner of instituting and administer-
> ing, a National Rehabilitation and Compensation
> Scheme appropriate to Australia, and which in
> principle the Australian Government has decided to
> establish, for the purpose of rehabilitating and
> compensating every person who at any time or in
> any place suffers a personal injury (including
> pre-natal injury) and whether the injury be
> sustained on the road, at work, in the home, in
> the school or elsewhere or is an industrial
> disease with particular reference to -
>
> (a) the circumstances in which an injury should
>   be covered:
>
> (b) the application of the scheme where death
>   results from the injury;
>
> (c) the nature and extent of the benefits that
>   should be provided;
>
> (d) how the scheme should be financed;
>
> (e) the relationship between benefits under the
>   scheme and other social service benefits;
>
> (f) whether rights under the scheme should be in
>   substitution for all or any rights now exist-
>   ing;
>
> (g) the encouragement of precautions against
>   accident;

(h) the provision of rehabilitation facilities;
     and

(i) the manner of administering the scheme.

1.202 <u>Sickness</u>. In some of the submissions made to
the committee it was argued that it is illogical to
distinguish between people who suffer some disability
as a result of injury and those who suffer similar
disabilities due to sickness. Accordingly, on 1st
February 1974 the terms of reference of the committee
were extended by the addition of the following
paragraph:

> And further to inquire into and report on an
> extension of the scheme for the purpose of
> rehabilitating and compensating every person who
> suffers a physical or mental incapacity or deform-
> ity by reason of sickness or congenital defect,
> together with the application of the scheme where
> death results from such sickness or defect.

1.203 It is to be noted that in the case of personal
injury (including pre-natal injury) the terms of
reference made it clear that the Australian Government
had in principle decided to establish a national
rehabilitation and compensation scheme. The committee's
function was in that case limited to inquiring into and
reporting on the scope and form of the scheme and how
it is to be instituted and administered. There was no
similar prior decision by the Government as to the
extension of the scheme to cover people disabled by
sickness.

1.204 In the result the committee did recommend the
extension of the scheme to sickness. It accepted that
in general no good reason existed for distinguishing
between similarly handicapped people according to the
cause of their disability. Only in certain minor
respects - notably with regard to the waiting period

for the commencement of benefits (see pars 4.205-6) and
the application of the scheme to non-residents (see par
3.403) - do the proposals make any such distinction.
Nevertheless, since the cost implications of the extension to sickness are very significant, the committee
drafted its detailed recommendations in such a way that
the injury-scheme could still be made fully operative
if the Government did not accept the recommendations
with regard to sickness.

1.205   Industrial Diseases. In this context it
should be observed that certain diseases - in particular
those resulting from the inhalation of dust in mines
and factories, such as asbestosis and silicoses - have
traditionally been compensated in the same way as
injuries. The original terms of reference included
"industrial disease" along with personal injury and the
proposed scheme retains this classification (see par
3.303). Thus the compensation of a disability stemming
from an industrial disease is to be treated throughout
in the same way as a disability resulting from personal
injury, not as a consequence of sickness.

Sec 3:   THE BASIC PRINCIPLES OF THE REPORT

1.301   The Problem. Nearly 7,000 Australians die
each year by accident. Over half of these are killed
in motor accidents. Injury statistics are not so easy
to obtain and figures for incapacitating illness are
still more difficult to find. (One product of the
implementation of the report will be the keeping of
uniform statistics so that henceforth we shall know the
true extent of the problem.) We do know that about
90,000 people annually suffer bodily injury requiring
medical or surgical treatment as a result of road
accidents. Although non-road work-accident statistics

are kept and published, the method is not uniform in
the various States. Thus in New South Wales injuries
are excluded if they result in less than three days'
incapacity, in Victoria and South Australia injuries
are excluded unless they result in incapacity for one
week, while in the other States any injury counts as
long as the incapacity prevents work for one day or
more. On these figures it appears that something like
170,000 people are injured at work. Thus over a
quarter of a million people are injured on the roads
and in the work-places of our industrialized society.
No statistics are available to show how many people in
Australia are injured in the home, on the sports field
and in other places of recreation, but these probably
exceed the numbers of whom we know. For the purpose of
estimating the cost of its proposed scheme the committee
had to turn to statistics of injuries and sickness
compiled in comparable overseas countries, though some
help with regard to seriously injured people was
obtained from hospital statistics in this country. In
the end the committee felt "able to say with confidence
that to the extent that there may be errors they
certainly do not lie on the side of under-estimation of
the costs of the proposals" (Report, Vol 1, par 491).

    1.302 No modern society can ignore the plight of the
injured and the sick. Often they are the victims of
the society's emphasis on production and fast transport.
Unwillingness to spend more on safer factory environ-
ments and good roads can hardly be blamed on the people
injured in consequence; if fault is to be attributed it
must be attributed to the whole community. In Australia
only a few can resist succumbing to the temptation of
"a few drinks with the mates", which so frequently ends
in disaster. Even if in some meaningful sense we can
blame the individual for bringing calamity on himself,

we have advanced beyond the stage where we wish to
visit the sins of the fathers on their wives and
children, whose needs are no less because the bread-
winner was careless for his own safety.

1.303 A primary aim of a modern society ought to be
to prevent as far as possible its members from becoming
disabled, whether from injury or sickness. Mass
immunization against disease and even compulsory chest
X-rays have for some years now proved acceptable. In
so far as we can prevent injuries, as well as sickness,
from occurring, the need for compensation does not
arise. The cost of improved road design and factory
lay-out can often be saved within a relatively short
time, not only in the smaller amount of compensation
required but also in increased productivity due to the
absence of disruption. Where we have failed, it is our
duty to attempt to remedy the failure by rehabilitation.
Again, in so far as we succeed in rehabilitating the
injured and the sick, the need for compensation is
diminished and productivity is increased. But there
will always remain a core of injuries which cannot be
eradicated; there will be deaths and severe disabilities where rehabilitation is impossible. In such
instances the community as a whole must bear the burden
of compensation.

1.304 Basic Principles. With this sort of
philosophy in mind the committee enunciated five
principles on which it based its proposed scheme.
These were: (1) community responsibility; (2) comprehensive entitlement; (3) complete rehabilitation; (4)
real compensation; and (5) administrative efficiency
(Report, Vol 1, pars 254-8).

1.305 <u>Community Responsibility</u>. The committee put forward three reasons for the acceptance of community responsibility. First, it spoke of "the civilised reasons of humanity". It apparently thought it unnecessary to elaborate on this. One would hope that compassion and concern for one's fellow-man who happened to be the victim of misfortune would now be widespread but there are still many people who, despite the sobering statistics of injury, adopt the attitude that "it couldn't happen to me" rather than "there but for the grace of God go I". For them, if they will not see that the suffering of individuals is due to the way the society is organized, not individual fault, perhaps the second reason may be more persuasive, viz "the economic reasons of self-interest". As the committee expressed it: "If the well-being of the work force is neglected the economy soon will suffer injury and society itself thus has much to lose." One should add that it is not only the actual members of the work force whose well-being must be cared for, but also that of the housewives who support them. Thirdly, since every member of the community would be covered by the scheme, every member must be prepared to contribute: "rights universally enjoyed must be accompanied by obligations universally accepted". Only a national, Australia-wide scheme could satisfy this principle.

1.306 Community responsibility for some of the injured has already been accepted as a result of the compulsory third party motor vehicle insurance schemes and compulsory workers' compensation throughout Australia and compulsory employers' liability insurance in some States. Every member of the community contributes either directly - by himself paying premiums - or indirectly - through the increased cost of goods and services - to providing a fund for the

compensation of victims of motor and work accidents.
Further evidence of the acceptance of community
responsibility has come recently from the addition to
compulsory third party motor insurance premiums in
Victoria and Tasmania of a component to provide limited
compensation for the victims of motor accidents on a
"no-fault" basis, so that now drivers and people they
innocently injure, as well as third parties who can
prove fault, have recourse to the insurance funds
derived from the community in those two States.
Criminal injury compensation schemes, now operating in
all States,[1] also bear witness to the willingness of
the community to accept responsibility for some of the
harm it fails to prevent.

1.307 A National Scheme. There are numerous draw-
backs, however, to the existing schemes. One relates
to absurd distinctions which are encountered as one
crosses State boundaries. A host of cases have come
before the courts because of the lack of uniformity
between the third party insurance legislation and the
fact that motorists refuse to stay within the borders
of their own States.[2] Variations in benefits under the
different workers' compensation Acts are considerable,
not only between States, but even within any one State
because of the existence of separate legislation
governing Commonwealth employees and others. The "de
facto wife" of a deceased worker may receive workers'
compensation in one State, but not in another, despite
the death having occurred in similar circumstances. A
Victorian who is criminally attacked may get

---

1. See W T Westling, "Some Aspects of the Judicial
   Determination of Compensation Payable to Victims
   of Crime in Australia" (1974) 48 ALJ 428.
2. A recent example in the High Court is Nominal
   Defendant v Morgan Cars Pty Ltd (1974) 3 ALR 33,
   48 ALJR 174.

compensation of up to $3,000 if he stayed at home, up to $4,000 if he was holidaying in New South Wales, but only a maximum of $1,000 if he was on a visit to South Australia. Thus a national scheme is imperative.

1.308 <u>Comprehensive Entitlement</u>. The main disadvantage of the present schemes is that they are piecemeal in operation. There is no lesser need merely because the injury, or sickness, occurs in circumstances not covered by the various systems. The dependants of a man killed while walking beside the road are no less deserving because his death was caused by the bite of a snake, rather than by the careless driving of a motorist. Yet at present there is usually no compensation of any sort payable in the one set of circumstances, though damages are recoverable in the other. A worker injured on his way to work is no more virtuous than the same worker injured on his way to visit a friend outside working hours. Yet the one is entitled to workers' compensation; the other is not. This is where the committee's second basic principle is important: the proposed scheme would provide <u>comprehensive</u> entitlement. There will be cover for all members of the community, including housewives, at all times and in all circumstances. This does not entail compensation for every trivial injury, but it means that where a real need is created by misfortune, all victims will be treated on an equal basis. (Consideration is given below to whether it is justifiable to distinguish, as the Bill does for the purposes of the date of commencement of benefits, between earners and non-earners and between earners injured in circumstances presently covered by workers' compensation and earners injured in other circumstances: see pars 4.207-8.)

1.309 Complete Rehabilitation. The third basic
philosophy - which indeed is described as the primary
objective of the scheme - is complete rehabilitation.
Every incapacitated person must be encouraged to
recover the maximum possible degree of bodily health,
vocational utility and social well-being as soon as
possible. The common law has too often achieved the
opposite. Rehabilitation is most effective when
measures towards it are undertaken swiftly, yet the
common law system, by withholding its lump-sum payment
for many years, has frequently denied the injured
person the means to embark on those measures. By
assessing the damages once and for all at a trial or
settlement years after the event, it has encouraged the
exaggeration of the disability. Such exaggeration may
not be conscious on the part of the injured person:
often it is a genuine psychological condition, or
"functional overlay", consequent on anxiety and brood-
ing during the lengthy period of waiting and uncertainty. The condition is aggravated by the plaintiff's
repetition of his symptoms to the numerous medical
experts engaged by his own solicitors and by the
insurance company on the other side.

1.310 Insurance companies have too often in the past
ignored their own self-interest by continuing regular
payments of workers' compensation without themselves
taking steps to find work for which injured persons are
fit.[3] With honourable exceptions[4] employers have too

---

3. Peluchetti v Warringah Brick & Pipe Works Pty Ltd
    [1961] NSWR 259 (FC) appears to be truly except-
    ional. There the injured worker was found
    employment as a lift-driver in the insurance
    company's building.
4. Cf the reference in Breska v Lysaghts Works Pty
    Ltd (1956) 74 WN (NSW) 168 (FC) to the commendable
    practice of BHP Co Ltd and its subsidiaries of

often shirked their own responsibility to their workers
and have regarded their own obligations as fulfilled
once an injured man is put "on compo" meted out by
their insurers. Governments, too, cannot be absolved
from blame in making inadequate facilities available to
cope with the demands of all those requiring rehabilitative treatment.

1.311 <u>Real Compensation</u>. While the common law and
workers' compensation, supplemented by no-fault motor
accident and criminal injury compensation schemes, make
adequate - and sometimes generous - provision for
people who happen to fall within their scope and who
suffer comparatively minor injuries, seriously injured
persons, even if entitled to the best that all these
schemes can offer, are seldom put back, so far as money
can do it, in the position they would have been in if
they had not been injured.[5] There are a number of
reasons for this failure. All the existing statutory
schemes are limited in the total amount payable, the
time for which payments are made, or both. Some
workers' compensation schemes do not attempt to relate
the weekly payments to the earnings lost. The common

---

providing work for men injured in their service.
See also <u>Smith</u> v <u>Australian Iron and Steel Ltd</u>
[1960] NSWR 501 (FC), 504 per Herron J. In
<u>Azzopardi</u> v <u>Nicholson Bros & Lucas Pty Ltd</u> [1962]
NSWR 1270 (FC), 1275, the exception was said by
Collins J to apply to "certain areas such as
Wollongong and Newcastle", rather than to partic-
ular employers.

5.   This is the avowed aim of common law damages:
Diplock LJ in <u>Fletcher</u> v <u>Autocar and Transporters</u>
[1968] 2 QB 322 (CA), 339, called it "a platitude".
Cf Menzies J in <u>Petroleum and Chemical Corporation</u>
<u>(Australia) Ltd</u> v <u>Morris</u> (1973) 47 ALJR 484, 485,
where he stated the principle as applicable to
"that part of damages for personal injury as
consists of lost earning capacity".

law, while unlimited except by the theoretical ability
of the defendant to pay,[6] has been unable to cope with
the problem of inflation and with the impossibility of
predicting accurately the future course of a plaintiff's
life. Furthermore, judges have been unwilling to make
full use of scientific assistance from actuaries and
have over-emphasized the adverse contingencies which
might have befallen the plaintiff if he had not been
injured. All of this has meant that lump-sum damages
have proved inadequate to replace even the financial
losses of the seriously injured in the long run. When
one takes into account also the effect of contributory
negligence on damages, it becomes apparent that
although the common law has lived up to its view that
"perfect compensation" is unattainable, it has fallen
far short of its ideal of "full and fair compensation".
(These criticisms are elaborated in pars 2.215-8.)

1.312 The Woodhouse scheme sets out to give every
incapacitated person the opportunity to maintain the
living standards he or she had previously achieved. It
does not impose any limits on the total amount of
compensation or the length of time for which it is
payable. Only a very high upper limit is set beyond
which earnings-related compensation for total incapacity
is not to go (see pars 4.210 and 4.214). It escapes
the straight-jacket into which the common law has been
forced by its adherence to the once-and-for-all lump-
sum award; instead it provides almost exclusively for
periodical payments (par 4.101). This ensures that
changes for the worse in the degree of incapacity can
be taken into account; though, in the interests of

---

6. See Lord Denning MR in Fletcher's case, supra, at
   335-6; Diplock LJ in Wise v Kaye [1962] 1 QB 638
   (CA), 669-70; and Lord Devlin in H West & Son Ltd
   v Shephard [1964] AC 326 (HL), 356-7.

rehabilitation, the scheme ignores changes for the
better once an incapacity has been declared permanent.
Inflation is taken care of by linking the various bases
for the calculation of entitlements, and the subsequent
benefits themselves, to appropriate indices (pars
4.701-5). The scheme makes no reduction for contingencies, though it does limit weekly benefits in the case
of total incapacity to 85 per cent of pre-injury
earnings. This deduction of 15 per cent is said to
represent the saving in transport and similar expenses
resulting from giving up work (Report, Vol 1, par
374(c)); in so far as it falls short of that saving it
provides an incentive to rehabilitation. The aims of
real compensation and complete rehabilitation are both
met by providing for the payment of expenses connected
with domiciliary care, such as the costs of ramps in
the home of a paraplegic and of a personal attendant
for a quadriplegic (Chap 4, Sec 5).

   1.313 Administrative Efficiency. Inherent in the
common law system is a wasteful expenditure of money.
Generally, no damages are payable at common law unless
the injured person can prove fault on the part of
another. Since the damages are seldom paid by the
person at fault, but by some insurance company or other
large organization, the investigation of fault serves
no useful purpose. In the case of compulsory motor
vehicle insurance the driver, if found to be at fault,
does not even lose a no-claim bonus or suffer an
increase in premiums and no insurer can refuse to
insure him because of his record. If he is prosecuted
criminally, there will in any event be an independent
inquiry into his conduct.

1.314 Yet, as the common law rewards a person who
can prove fault, many injured people try to do so.
Such attempts, whether successful or not, are extremely
costly to the community. Investigators have to be
employed in many cases to determine how the accident
happened. Experts from many fields are then sometimes
called in to theorize as to whether such things as a
broken steering shaft were the cause or consequence of
the accident. Solicitors and barristers are engaged.
Scarce medical resources are then used up, not for the
purpose of healing the injured, but to assess the
extent of their disability and to predict its future
course. All this is duplicated because of the adversary
nature of the proceedings, which requires both plaintiff
and defendant to have their own expert witnesses and
lawyers. Finally, although only a small percentage of
cases are not settled and actually reach trial, where
the disputed issues can really be determined, the time
of the courts is taken up to an inordinate extent by
personal injury actions. This involves not only the
appointment of many more judges, court officials,
shorthand writers, etc than would otherwise be the case,
but still in some jurisdictions - like Victoria - the
summoning from the community of dozens of jurors each
week, each of whom has to forgo his or her normal
activities for a period, whether or not he or she is
actually selected to hear a case.

1.315 The common law, being wedded to the once-and-
for-all lump-sum concept of damages, discouraged
plaintiffs from seeking a speedy settlement of their
claim, lest what appears to be an inconsequential

injury take an unexpected turn for the worse.[7]   The
adverse effect on rehabilitation of waiting until the
injury has "stabilized" has already been noted.   If the
injury does not fall within the workers' compensation
or no-fault motor accident schemes, considerable hardship can be caused to the plaintiff and his family in
the interim.   In the past the acceptance of workers'
compensation barred the plaintiff from his common law
remedy, but today the vestiges of the doctrines of
"election" and "recovery" have steadily been eroded.
Nevertheless, the limited periods for which those
benefits are payable often mean that plaintiffs are
left destitute long before their cases are ready for
trial.[8]   Pressure to settle on unfavourable terms is
considerable.   Charity and social security are unlikely
to be adequate to tide the plaintiff over until the
golden apple of common law damages is ripe for plucking.
Even if he is able to wait, the fruit may be snatched
from his grasp because the court determines that he is
not able to prove that the defendant was at fault; or
he may be allowed only a small bite because he is found
to have been contributorily negligent.

   1.316   All this occurs in a context of an adversary
nature.   The defendant may be told by his insurers not
even to enquire after the health of his victim for fear
that he will let slip an inadvertent admission which

---

7.   In Fetter v Beal (1701) 1 Ld Raym 339, which laid
     down the once-and-for-all rule, the Court blamed
     the plaintiff for having been too hasty in bring-
     ing his first action; had he waited he could also
     have recovered for the operation which became
     necessary.
8.   The cold statistics of delay in settlement set out
     in the Compendium, Part IV, Table 9 (see par
     5.106) are given heart-rending human content in
     Appendix II of the submission to the committee by
     the Australian Council of Social Service.

could be used by the plaintiff in the court proceedings.
A plaintiff injured at work cannot even have a frank
discussion with his employer's safety officer with a
view to preventing such accidents befalling his work-
mates in the future: each party must be on his guard
not to prejudice the possible outcome of the court case.

1.317   The answers which the Woodhouse report
proposes to the inefficiency of the common law are to
do away with lump sums, to provide for speedy assessment, to allow for interim payments and to discourage
adversary proceedings.

1.318   Costs.   It has long been surmised that the
common law system, as it applies to motor accidents, is
expensive in terms of the proportion of each dollar of
premium income which does not find its way into the
pockets of victims.   (This way of looking at the matter
does not take account of many of the hidden costs
referred to in pars 1.314-5.)   In the Report (Vol 1,
pars 153-4) the committee purports to contrast
unfavourably the costs of administering the compulsory
motor vehicle insurance schemes in Australia with the
costs of administering the State-run workers' compensation scheme in Ontario.   Unfortunately, the figures
given do not enable a proper comparison to be made,
although there can be little doubt that the Ontario
scheme is cheaper.   It is stated that the overall cost
associated with the assessment and distribution of
compensation in Ontario is about 7 per cent of premiums.
Table V sets out legal costs (presumably including
medical and other expert witness fees, but excluding
plaintiff's solicitor-and-client costs) in three
Australian States as a percentage of net payments (ie
total payments less claimants' party-and-party costs).
These percentages range from 18.1 in South Australia to

26.9 in Victoria, but since they are percentages of net
payments, not of premiums, the direct comparison which
paragraph 154 of the Report makes with Ontario appears
to be false.

1.319   The number of insurers willing to participate
in the compulsory motor vehicle insurance schemes in
Australia has been steadily declining in recent years.
Premiums, which are generally fixed by statutory bodies,
often lag behind the true costs of the system, and,
though insurers may well be saved commissions and
collection expenses as a result of the work done by the
motor vehicle registration boards, this area of
insurance has probably ceased to be profitable.   Even
if figures had been obtained showing the percentage of
total premiums which goes to administration, owing to
the many hidden costs of the fault system a comparison
with the Ontario experience would not have been very
meaningful.

1.320   Fuller information is revealed in the Report
about the costs of the Australian employers' liability
schemes, which encompass both workers' compensation and
common law liability.   Nevertheless, the direct
comparison made in paragraph 200 of Volume 1 with the
Ontario position seems again to be untenable.   From the
Compendium, Part 6, to take only the Victorian figures,
it appears that in 1971-72, 19.5 per cent of premiums,
or 43.7 per cent of net benefits paid, went into
management and commission expenses.   When legal costs
on both sides (other than plaintiffs' solicitor-and-
client costs) are added in, the figures become 26.2 per
cent of premiums, or 58.6 per cent of net benefits.
Since, however, premiums were $83,624,000, expenses and
legal costs $21,871,000 and net benefits $37,294,000,
this leaves $24,459,000, or 29.2 per cent of premiums,
unaccounted for.   Presumably this last amount went into

profits and reserves. Overall, it seems that only 44.5
per cent of premiums found its way back to injured
people (and even some of that had to be paid in
solicitor-and-client fees). When one considers,
however, that the premiums which provided the fund for
payment of benefits in 1971-72 should in fact have been
collected in earlier years - and the total amount so
collected would certainly have been lower in each of
those years than in 1971-72 - the picture might not be
quite so dismal. Nevertheless, little doubt can remain
that the system is very expensive compared with, say,
the costs of administering the hospital and medical
benefit funds in Australia, where expenses are less
than 16 per cent of premiums.[9] Where the Australian
Government uses its tax-gathering powers on a uniform
basis, the costs, at least of collection, should be
reduced still further.

Sec 4:   THE BILL

1.401   Ho<u>use of Representatives</u>. As already
mentioned Volume 1 of the <u>Report</u> contained a draft Bill
designed to give effect to the recommendations of the
committee with regard to compensation. The Government
lost very little time in introducing the National
Compensation Bill, with only a few amendments, into the
House of Representatives. During the course of its
passage through the lower House, many amendments were
made to the Bill, most of which were concerned with the

---

9.   The Annual Reports of the Directors-General of
     Health and Social Security, tabled in Parliament
     pursuant to s 76A of the National Health Act, show
     management expenses of hospital benefit funds on a
     nation-wide basis at under 8 per cent and of
     medical benefit funds on a similar basis at under
     16 per cent.

staged introduction of the different parts of the
scheme relating to injury and sickness (see Chap 3, Sec
2).

1.402 Senate. When the Bill came before the Senate
for its second reading, it was agreed by all parties
that it should be referred to the upper House's
Standing Committee on Constitutional and Legal Affairs
for consideration and report. The date by which the
Standing Committee was to report back was originally
fixed at 30 November 1974. The Standing Committee
publicly invited submissions on the Bill. In view of
the response, it became obvious that full consideration
could not be given to the matter within the time
permitted. Accordingly, the Senate extended the time
in which the Standing Committee is to report to 30th
April 1975.

1.403 Assumptions. This survey is being written
concurrently with the consideration of the Bill by the
Senate's Standing Committee. At the time of writing
it is not known whether the Standing Committee will
report favourably or unfavourably on the general terms
of the Bill. It is known that the Government has
indicated that it is prepared to listen sympathetically
to submissions concerning anomalies in the Bill and
that it will introduce amendments to any provisions
shown to be unfair. Thus the Bill as described hereafter is not necessarily in its final form. Whether
that final form will be approved by the Senate as a
whole and so pass into law can only be a matter of
conjecture. Hereafter in this book it will be assumed
that the Bill will be enacted in the form in which it
stood at the date of its referral to the Senate
Standing Committee. Accordingly, clauses of the Bill
will be referred to throughout as sections of the Act.

It should be borne in mind, however, that changes are possible, indeed likely, not only by way of amendments to the Bill, but thereafter by amending Acts, before the first part of the scheme starts operating on 1st July 1976.

Chapter 2

THE PRESENT LAW

Sec 1: A PLETHORA OF SYSTEMS

2.101   In setting out the basic philosophy of the
Woodhouse Report (Chap 1, Sec 3), it has been necessary
to make some reference to the existing law to indicate
the mischief which the National Compensation Act is
designed to overcome. It is now proposed to sketch a
little more fully, though still not in great detail,
the existing provisions for the compensation of injured
people in Australia.

2.102   Available Schemes. Depending on the circumstances, a victim of injury may fall under one or more
of the following schemes: (a) He may have an action
for damages at common law. (b) He may be entitled to
workers' compensation. (c) If he is injured in
Victoria or Tasmania, he may receive no-fault motor
accident benefits. (d) He may come within the scope of
a criminal injuries compensation scheme. (e) He may be
eligible for social security payments. Or he may find
himself outside all these schemes and be left to bear
his entire loss himself or with the assistance of
charity. Even if he does receive benefits from one or
more of these schemes, his losses might easily exceed
the limits of compensation so recoverable.

2.103   Fortuitous Circumstances of Injury. An
illustration of the fortuitous way in which the schemes
operate from the point of view of the victim may be

readily given. Suppose that a man, while at work in
Victoria, suddenly runs amok. He seizes a bottle and
hits a fellow-worker over the head with it. He then
runs outside where he picks up a spade, with which he
strikes a gardener. Afterwards he climbs into a motor
car and runs down some children playing on the footpath.
Thereafter, he leaves the car and attacks some other
children with the spade, which he still has.
Eventually, when threatening a further victim, he is
himself shot and killed by a policeman.

   2.104 It may be that all the victims of the man who
ran amok would have a claim against his estate for
damages at common law. This is not certain, since
there are few authoritative statements of the common
law liability of insane persons;[1] the question might be
settled only after an expensive appeal to the High
Court of Australia or even to the Privy Council in
England. Assuming, as is probably the case, that the
estate is liable to pay common law damages, it may well
be that there are inadequate assets in it to meet all
the claims. Thus the theoretical right of the victims
to recover common law damages might prove worthless -
except in one instance: the children run down by the
car will be better off than the other victims. This is
because, if there is common law liability for bodily
injury arising out of the use of a motor vehicle,
compulsory motor vehicle insurance will see to it that
there is a solvent fund available to pay the damages.
Even if there is no common law liability, the children
injured by the use of the motor car will be better off
than those injured with the spade, since in Victoria
there are now no-fault benefits payable under the Motor
Accidents Act 1972.

---

1.   See J G Fleming, The Law of Torts (4th ed, 1971),
     23-4.

2.105 In Victoria all the victims of the beserk
assailant would be entitled also to compensation, up to
a maximum of $3,000, assessed in the same way as common
law damages, under the Criminal Injuries Compensation
Act 1972. This Act specifically provides for payment
cf compensation notwithstanding that the assailant
might be acquitted of a criminal charge on the grounds
of insanity. The fellow-worker injured, since the
assault on him occurred in the course of his employment,
is entitled to workers' compensation. The gardener may
or may not be entitled to workers' compensation. In
his case it will depend on whether he is classified as
an employee or an independent contractor, a distinction
which is not always easy to make and which has given
rise to much litigation. If the man who ran amok had a
wife and children dependent on him, they would appear
to be remediless unless they satisfied the means test
and became eligible for social security benefits.

2.106 Consequences of Circumstances. It is exceedingly difficult to justify this differential treatment
for all the equally innocent victims of similar
misfortune. It becomes impossible when one remembers
that the benefits, and in particular the maximum amount
recoverable, depend not on the needs of the individual
victim, but on the particular scheme he happens to fall
under. Thus the common law damages, if recoverable,
are unlimited; workers' compensation under the Workers
Compensation Act 1958 (Vic), as amended to 1974, could,
in the most exceptional circumstances, amount to nearly
$29,000 (nearly $14,000 by way of lump sum and a little
over $15,000 in periodical payments); the Motor
Accidents Act benefits for loss of earnings are limited
to $12,480 (in addition medical expenses are payable
under this and the Workers Compensation Act); criminal
injuries compensation is, as we have seen, limited in

Victoria to $3,000; and social security payments are
exiguous.   These discrepancies are multiplied when one
takes into the picture the other five States and two
Territories, as well as the Commonwealth Employees
Compensation Schemes.

2.107 Duplication. It will have been noticed that
in some instances a particular victim is eligible for
benefits in respect of the same injury under more than
one of the existing schemes. The interaction of the
various schemes has given rise to much difficulty.
Although on the whole duplication of benefits is
avoided, this is not always the case. It has for many
years been the practice, where a man is killed in
circumstances entitling his dependants to bring an
action for damages under the legislation in all States
derived from the English Fatal Accidents Act 1846
(Lord Campbell's Act) and also to workers' compensation,
for the eldest child alone to claim workers' compensation, while the rest of the family seeks damages, thus
effectively increasing the total benefit to the family.
On the other hand, where duplication is avoided, it is
sometimes at the cost of considerable unfairness, as
was the case where the "election" or "recovery" of
workers' compensation, however scanty, precluded
subsequent common law action.[2] Legislation drafted to
avoid duplication is often exceedingly difficult to
interpret.[3]

2.108 Workers' Compensation. The scope of workers'
compensation in Australia has been progressively

---

2. Eg Smith v Commonwealth Oil Refineries Ltd (1938)
    60 CLR 141.
3. It may be expected that s 79 of the Motor
    Accidents Act 1972 (Vic) will lead to litigation
    before its meaning is settled. Ss 63 and 79 of
    the Workers Compensation Act 1958 (Vic) have
    recently been the subject of a report by the Chief
    Justice's Law Reform Committee.

expanded. Stemming from late 19th century legislation
in the United Kingdom (since abandoned in that country)
which made an employer liable to compensate a worker
suffering personal injury by accident arising out of
and in the course of his employment, statutes in force
in Australia today are considerably broader in scope.
Thus, everywhere except in Tasmania, it is today enough
if the injury arose out of or in the course of employment. Further, cover has been extended to "journey
injuries", suffered on the way to or from work and a
host of other places. Litigation frequently arises as
to whether a worker is covered when he is injured while
living at home within the environs of his work.[4] Even
apart from such instances, the coverage of the various
Acts bristles with anomalies. One may illustrate by
assuming a series of pairs of people injured in circumstances identical for each member of the pair in each
case except for one fact. A and B are both injured in
an explosion at a factory; A is employed there; B at
the time is unemployed and is seeking work: A is
covered, B is not. C is mowing the lawn on one
property, D is mowing the lawn on the property next
door when each unintentionally cuts off his own big
toe; C is an employee; D is an independent contractor:
C is covered, D is not. E, riding on the tram, is on
his way to work; F, sitting next to him, intends to go
shopping as it is his day off: E is covered; F is not.[5]
G, fielding at mid-on, is playing cricket away from his
place of employment during his lunch-hour; H, fielding

4. A recent example is <u>Mason</u> v <u>Social Welfare Depart-
    ment</u> [1974] VR 506 (FC).
5. The following examples are based on actual cases
    in the law reports. They were set out in an
    article by the present writer in (1966) 40 ALJ
    179. Footnotes to the original article identify
    the cases.

at mid-off, is whiling away time between shifts: G is
covered; H is not.   K is proprietor of a small business;
L has sold his business to his own private company and
has entered into a contract of employment with the
company: K is not covered, but L is.   M, employed by
the Commonwealth Government, loses a leg; N, employed
by the State Government, loses his leg: the compensation payable to each may vary.   Many more examples
could be given.

2.109   Conclusion.   By now it should have been
adequately demonstrated that the existing systems for
the compensation of injured people are in need of
drastic overhaul in the interests of comprehensive
coverage and uniform entitlement.   Before considering
in detail the alternative offered by the National
Compensation Act, one should, however, pay some
attention to the common law, as bequeathed to us by the
wisdom of judges rather than legislators (though
legislation has not been completely absent in this
field).

Sec 2:   THE COMMON LAW

2.201   Fault.   Although remedies for injury to the
person go back deep into the roots of the common law in
the 12th and 13th centuries, the basic system applied
in the courts today became fully developed in the 19th
century.   In that age of sturdy individualism the
catch-cry was "no liability without fault".   A person
sustaining a personal injury was left to bear his own
loss as best he could, unless he could prove that the
cause of the injury was the fault of another.   Such
fault provided, in the eyes of the common law judges, a
good reason for shifting the loss from the innocent
victim to the guilty wrongdoer.

2.202 Strict Liability. Yet even in the 19th
century "no liability without fault" was never
completely accepted as a universal truth. The ancient
remedy for cattle trespass, for instance, whereby a
farmer could be made liable to his neighbour for failing to keep his livestock within his own bounds, was
not dependent on fault. In the mid-nineteenth century
the courts invented a new tort which made the occupier
liable for the escape from his land of a dangerous
substance - such as water in unnatural quantities -
which he collected on it, though he personally took all
reasonable care to prevent such escape. Both these
torts have in the 20th century been held to give a
remedy for personal injury.[1] Injuries caused by wild
animals, or domesticated ones known to be vicious, have
always rendered their keepers strictly liable; modern
statutes in Australia have extended this liability so
as to deprive dogs of even their first bite or snap.[2]

2.203 Defences. Nor did the converse of the maxim
"no liability without fault" apply with any consistency
in the 19th century. "Fault" might have been very easy
to demonstrate in the primitive safety conditions
prevalent in the factories. Conscious perhaps that
burgeoning industry would be suppressed if the
entrepreneurs were required to bear the true cost of
their products, including the blood of the workers and
their mangled limbs, the judges of the 19th century
steadfastly applied an "unholy trinity" of defences of
their own invention. The doctrine of common employment
precluded a worker from suing his employer where his
injury was due to the fault of a fellow-worker;

---

1. Wormald v Cole [1954] 1 QB 614 (CA); Benning v
    Wong (1969) 122 CLR 249.
2. See generally J G Fleming, The Law of Torts (4th
    ed, 1971), 302-8; Dog Act 1970 (Vic), s 22.

contributory negligence on the part of the plaintiff,
however trivial, deprived him of the whole of the
judgment to which he was otherwise entitled; and the
maxim volenti non fit injuria, or voluntary assumption
of risk, was given free reign though it must have been
obvious that the factory employee had no real choice in
the matter. It should not be forgotten that late in
the 19th century workers' compensation legislation had
to be introduced because of the inadequacy of the
common law in providing a remedy for injured employees.

2.204 Eventually it required legislation to abolish
the defence of common employment.[3] The courts
contorted themselves in an effort to escape the
shackles of contributory negligence,[4] but again
legislation was necessary to mitigate the harshness of
the defence.[5] To a large extent volenti non fit
injuria was eventually successfully contained in
employer-employee cases by decisions of the courts
themselves, though even there its ghost has not been
completely laid.[6] In the area of the liability of a
driver of a car to his passenger, and also in occupiers'
liability, it continues to give trouble.[7] Advocates of
the retention of the common law are hardly likely to
want it in its pristine 19th century form.

2.205 Death. It should also not be forgotten that
the common law courts turned their faces against allowing an action for the death of a human being. Again,
legislatures had to step in to provide a remedy in the

---

3. Eg Employers and Employés Act 1958 (Vic), s 34.
4. Eg Alford v Magee (1952) 85 CLR 437.
5. Eg Wrongs Act 1958 (Vic), Part V.
6. ICI Ltd v Shatwell [1965] AC 656 (HL); cf Burnett
    v British Waterways Board [1973] 2 All ER 631 (CA).
7. See Fleming, op cit, 244-6; Ashdown v Samuel
    Williams & Sons [1957] 1 QB 409 (CA) and White v
    Blackmore [1972] 2 QB 651 (CA).

form of an action brought to compensate certain close relatives for their loss. It was the courts, too, which restrictively interpreted the statutes as encompassing only financial loss, not grief or sorrow.

2.206 **Breach of Statutory Duty.** Another respect in which the common law has been supplemented results from the proliferation of industrial safety regulations now governing matters such as the fencing of machinery, the stability of scaffolding and the provision of protective clothing. Although in form most of these regulations provide only for criminal sanctions for their breach, the courts have shown a willingness to interpret them as giving also a civil remedy to a worker injured in consequence. A worker who succeeds in an action for breach of statutory duty is entitled to have his damages assessed in the same way as if he had proved fault at common law. Often the liability imposed on the employer is absolute and absence of fault is no defence. From the point of view of the innocent worker it can be purely fortuitous whether or not he finds himself within the scope of a statutory duty.[8]

2.207 **Negligence.** Despite the instances of strict liability referred to in paragraphs 2.202 and 2.206, it remains true that for success in most common law actions, particularly those arising out of motor vehicle accidents, the plaintiff must prove fault. Apart from the rare cases of intentional harm, this means that the plaintiff must show that the defendant was negligent. The test for negligence is objective:

8. See the note by B A Hepple in [1974] Cam LJ 37, where he castigates as "unfair and illogical" the contrasting results in Westwood v PO [1974] AC 1 (HL) and Haigh v Charles W Ireland Ltd [1974] 1 WLR 43 (HL).

whether the defendant failed to do something a reasonable man would have done, or did something which a
reasonable man would not have. Thus there may be no
moral blame attributable to the defendant: it is no
excuse in an action for damages at common law that he
was born hasty, clumsy or awkward and was unable to
help doing what he did. It has been held in a case at
first instance that the driver of a car afflicted with
a mental illness is not to be excused on that account:
Adamson v MVIT (1957) 58 WALR 56. On the other hand, a
motorist who suffers a sudden heart-attack causing him
to lose control of his vehicle would not be liable:
the reasonable man is never mentally ill, though he may
be physically! Whether an innocent pedestrian recovers
damages can turn on whether the driver was stung by a
bee or by a taunt from one of his passengers.

2.208 The standard of care required, though objective in the sense described above, is an elusive one.
Time and again appellate courts have set aside findings
of negligence by juries on the ground that there was no
evidence of a failure to take reasonable care.[9] In the
absence of juries appellate courts are frequently
divided among themselves on whether or not negligence
has been established, so that it is not uncommon to find
that a majority of all the judges who considered a
particular case were in favour of one party, but the
other party succeeded because he was able to command a
majority in the highest court.[10] When contributory
negligence is also in issue, the permutations sometimes

9.   Eg Vozza v Tooth & Co Ltd (1964) 112 CLR 316.
10. Eg Paris v Stepney BC [1951] AC 367 (HL); cf
     MLC Assurance Co Ltd v Evatt [1971] AC 793 (PC),
     a negligence case not involving personal injury.

become ludicrous, though for the plaintiff they can be tragic.[11]

2.209 Further difficulties are introduced by the fact that the trial of a negligence action is not likely to occur much less than three years after the events giving rise to the claim, and often after a much longer interval. Even if the trial were held immediately afterwards, the fallibility of eye-witnesses as to what happened in perhaps a split second could give little confidence that the truth would emerge. When given years later, the evidence must raise serious doubts as to its reliability. On the acceptance of what witnesses now say happened in a motor collision years ago depends whether the plaintiff recovers perhaps many thousands of dollars or nothing. All these uncertainties fully justify the description of the negligence action as a "forensic lottery". (*The Forensic Lottery* is the title of a book by T G Ison, published in 1967, which advocates the replacement of the tort system by a scheme such as that subsequently proposed by the Woodhouse committee. See also M A Franklin, "Replacing the Negligence Lottery" (1967) 53 Virginia L Rev 774.)

2.210 In most motor and industrial accidents the uncertainties are factual. Other areas of negligence law introduce uncertainty as to the very rules to be applied. The liability of occupiers to entrants on their land has led in recent years to no fewer than three appeals to the Privy Council from Australian courts and numerous appeals to other appellate

---

. 11. See the writer's discussion of <u>Da Costa</u> v <u>Cockburn Salvage & Trading Pty Ltd</u> (1970) 124 CLR 192 in (1971) 45 ALJ 312.

courts;[12] and yet the law cannot be regarded as clearly
settled. Liability for animals straying on to the
highway - for long the subject of a special immunity in
England until abolished by statute - remains doubtful
in Australia.[13] The traditional immunity of highway
authorities in respect of the failure to repair road
surfaces under their control has been qualified by
exceptions of uncertain extent.[14] Another immunity -
that of vendor or lessor for defects in buildings - has
come under increasing attack, but the success of the
assault is still unknown.[15] Little guidance is to be
gained from the case-law on the attenuation of the duty
of care owed to persons engaged in unlawful conduct.[16]
Despite liberalization of the protection given to
specially sensitive people, the law cannot be taken to
be authoritatively determined;[17] nor is the isolated
Australian decision[18] on the duty to the unborn
necessarily the final word on the matter.

   2.211 Insurance. The common law of negligence, with
all its imperfections, was intelligible in the context
of a suit between an individual victim and an individual
by whom he had been injured. Justice seemed to require

---

12. Commissioner for Railways v Quinlan [1964] AC 1054
     (PC); Commissioner for Railways v McDermott [1967]
     1 AC 169 (PC); Southern Portland Cement Ltd v
     Cooper [1974] AC 623; Fleming, op cit, Chap 19;
     and see Schiller v Mulgrave Shire Council (1972)
     46 ALJR 650, noted (1974) 9 MULR 550.
13. See Hill v Clarke (1969) 91 WN (NSW) 550 (CA).
14. Fleming, op cit, 361-5.
15. See Voli v Inglewood Shire Council (1963) 110 CLR
     74, 91; Dutton v Bognor Regis UDC [1972] 1 QB 373
     (CA).
16. See (1970) 44 ALJ 280.
17. Cf Chester v Waverley Corporation (1939) 62 CLR 1
     with Mt Isa Mines Ltd v Pusey (1970) 125 CLR 383
     and Haley v London Electricity Board [1965] AC 778
     (HL).
18. Watt v Rama [1972] VR 353 (FC).

that if the victim could prove fault on the part of the
defendant, the loss should be shifted; if he could not
prove fault, then the loss had to lie where it fell.
Since perfect justice was unattainable in human courts,
the closest approximation had to suffice. All this was
falsified by the growth of liability insurance. Those
who were likely to do injury, rather than those who
were likely to suffer it, became conscious of the risk
and were able to take steps to avoid it. Liability
insurance became far more common than personal accident
insurance. When the motor vehicle accident toll was
growing to intolerable proportions, legislatures made
such liability insurance compulsory. Some Australian
statutes have done the same with employers' liability.

2.212 Today negligence actions are rarely between
individual plaintiffs and individual defendants, whatever the form they take. Behind the defendant almost
invariably stands an insurance company or similar
organization able to spread the cost of any judgment
among the thousands or even millions who benefit from
the defendant's activity. In the case of compulsory
motor vehicle insurance the individual defendant does
not suffer in any way from a finding of liability:
there are no no-claim bonuses to be lost or increased
premiums to be paid in consequence. The fault of the
defendant seems an irrelevant criterion for the shifting of the loss from the victim to the insurance fund
when the wrongdoer no longer pays personally. Two
pedestrians are run down by two motor cars: why should
the key to the coffers of the insurance fund be available to one who can prove that the driver of the car
which ran him down was negligent, while the other has
to fall back on other remedies, if any, because a tyre
on the car which ran him down burst without warning?

2.213 Deterrence. A possible reason for the
emphasis on fault in the 19th century was the view that
by imposing liability only when the defendant was at
fault, future conduct of that sort would be prevented.
There is little empirical evidence that negligent
conduct can be deterred by the threat of liability to
pay damages. In certain fields, such as product-
liability, it may even be true that strict liability -
far from being useless to prevent accidents - would be
more effective, since it would make potential defendants
even more careful to avoid the accidents which are
avoidable but which the plaintiff cannot prove are due
to negligence. Be that as it may, any deterrent effect
of the negligence action is removed by liability
insurance, especially where premiums cannot be adjusted
in consequence. The danger of injury to himself must
surely be the most potent deterrent to the driver of a
motor car. If that is insufficient, it can always be
supplemented by criminal penalties.

2.214 The most effective way of reducing accidents
is to attain a true understanding of their causes. We
have outgrown the mediaeval philosophy that disease is
a punishment from God for immoral behaviour and we have,
by immunization or the use of anti-biotics, eliminated
many of the epidemic illnesses after studying the
nature of micro-organisms. So we need proper studies
of the aetiology of accidents, rather than spurious
investigations into fault. [19] As has already been
observed, the truth is not likely to come out when
immediately the accident has occurred the protagonists

19. This analogy is put forward by Mr E C Wigglesworth
     of the injury research project of the Royal
     Australasian College of Surgeons. The committee
     agreed that the analogy is apt (Report, Vol 1,
     par 427; Vol 2, par 304).

are placed in an adversary posture, not daring to make admissions as to what happened.

2.215 <u>Damages</u>.[20] The aim of damages at common law is to restore the plaintiff, so far as money can do so, to the position he would have been in if he had not been injured. Although perfect restitution is impossible, the law seeks to award a fair and moderate sum to compensate the plaintiff for the injury sustained. In so far as the injury creates new needs, such as for medical, hospital or nursing attention or for wheelchairs or artificial limbs, the costs can be calculated in money terms with reasonable certainty. Loss of income, too, is commensurable with the compensation payable, though here there is always uncertainty as to what fate would have befallen the plaintiff if he had not been injured and often uncertainty as to what he will be capable of earning in his present state. In the realm of non-pecuniary loss - pain and suffering, loss of amenities, loss of expectation of life and disfigurement - the Australian courts, in refusing to recognize a "tariff" like that in England, have been unable to offer much guidance.

2.216 One might concede that so far as concerns less serious injuries, there is no apparent dissatisfaction with the methods of assessing damages at common law. Most such cases are settled and the outcome of the bargaining process is probably to reimburse the plaintiff for his financial loss and to give him something of a <u>solatium</u> for his inconvenience.[21] But a

---

20. For a full exposition see H Luntz, <u>The Assessment of Damages for Personal Injury and Death</u> (1974).
21. It may be doubted whether Australian plaintiffs are better informed of their rights to damages for non-pecuniary loss than the surprisingly ignorant Americans surveyed in J O'Connell and R Simon,

number of studies have shown that the seriously
incapacitated plaintiff fares very badly. Delays in
bringing such cases to trial are greater and the
pressure to settle for inadequate sums proportionately
increased. When the cases do come to trial, the common
law rules that the damages must be assessed once and
for all and must be awarded in a lump sum have proved
inadequate to cope with the problems inherent in predicting the future. In particular, the accelerating
rate of inflation has shown to be disastrous the rule
comparatively recently laid down by the High Court of
Australia in O'Brien v McKean (1968) 118 CLR 540 that
future increased earnings and expenses due to inflation
are to be ignored in the absence of a sort of evidence
not likely to be available in the practical world. The
Woodhouse Report sets out in Appendix 6 to Volume 1 a
letter from the mother of a paraplegic girl who in 1965
was awarded a record sum of damages in the New South
Wales Supreme Court (Thurston v Todd [1965] NSWR 1158;
on appeal [1966] 1 NSWR 321 (CA)). In 1974 the mother
wrote: "The total amount of damages has been invested
and at present returns a gross income of $10,514, but
this is completely absorbed by nursing and medical
expenses which amounted to $10,792 last year and with
increased wages has already increased since."

2.217 Medical prognosis, on which the courts are
compelled to rely, is obviously unreliable. There are
said to be many people living today who, on the evidence
given at the trial of their actions for damages, should
now be dead. Where they have outlived their predicted
life-span, damages awarded to provide for their needs
must necessarily be inadequate, even without an erosion

Payment for Pain and Suffering: Who Wants What,
When and Why (1972).

in the value of money. When confronted with a potential case of traumatic epilepsy or osteoarthritis,
doctors can do no more than estimate the chance of the
condition developing. If it does, the plaintiff is
likely to be under-compensated; if it does not he may
receive something of a windfall. No one can predict
with any degree of success how long a widow will remain
unmarried,[22] yet the determination of the amount of
damages to which she is entitled for the death of her
husband is dependent on that inherently uncertain fact.

2.218 Uncertainty as to what will be is bad enough;
uncertainty as to what might have been is probably
worse. Actuarial evidence can, however, be helpful in
valuing the lost earning capacity of the plaintiff,[23]
but the courts have shown a reluctance to use it
directly, preferring to rely heavily on their own
instinct, to which the actuarial figures are said to
offer no more than a "guide". The adverse contingencies to which we are all subject are often emphasized,
while favourable ones are only occasionally remarked
upon. In consequence the damages awarded are almost
certainly discounted too greatly because of the
possibility of other misfortune having befallen the
plaintiff if he had not been injured.

2.219 _Contributory Negligence_. Attention has
already been called to the fact that it was necessary
for legislatures to remedy the harsh all-or-nothing
effect of the defence of contributory negligence at
common law. Had that amendment of the law come at a
time when the contest was between an individual

---

22. See the analysis of remarriage statistics by
    Moffitt J A in _Schiffmann_ v _Jones_ (1970) 70 SR
    (NSW) 455 (CA), 463-9.
23. The latest article on the point is by P C Wickens,
    "Actuarial Assistance in Assessing Damages" (1974)
    48 ALJ 286.

plaintiff and an individual defendant it would rightly
have been welcomed as doing justice. In so far as a
plaintiff contributed to his own injury, it was fair
for him to bear the burden of the loss rather than the
defendant. But the reform came too late, at a time
when already the defendant was much better able to
distribute the loss than the plaintiff. Assume that a
plaintiff suffers $10,000 worth of damages and is
adjudged to be 50 per cent responsible. The defendant's
share, $5,000, is widely distributed through insurance
or the cost of the defendant's products and services;
the plaintiff's share of $5,000 is concentrated on
himself alone. An increase in the defendant's
responsibility to 60 per cent will mostly make little
difference to him; an increase in the plaintiff's
responsibility to 60 per cent can be calamitous,
depriving him not only of all his compensation for non-
pecuniary loss but eating more and more vigorously into
his financial losses. A survey carried out by the
Woodhouse committee revealed that in cases of death and
permanent disability damages were reduced for contributory negligence in 20.5 per cent in New South Wales,
21.3 per cent in South Australia, 28.3 per cent in
Victoria and 27.1 per cent in Queensland (Report, Vol 1,
Table III). The average reduction of damages in all
cases, serious and non-serious, where contributory
negligence applied, was 39.5 per cent (Report, Vol 1,
Table IV). Of the total of $850, 282 assessed damages
in the cases in the survey, $335,917 was deducted for
contributory negligence (ibid) and therefore had to be
borne by the plaintiffs themselves.

2.220 Moreover, the apportionment of damages on account of contributory negligence is haphazard in its application.[24] Assume A and B each steps off the footpath into the road without taking reasonable care for his own safety and that each is injured by a negligent motorist in circumstances where his damages fall to be reduced by 50 per cent. A luckily suffers only a graze and his damages are assessed at $100. B strikes his head on the kerb as he falls, suffering brain damage; his damages are assessed at $100,000. For similar instances of momentary negligence, A is "penalized" to an amount of $50, whereas B loses $50,000. Or assume that A and B are both seriously injured, so that damages in each case would be assessed at $100,000. A, however, is run down by C, who is driving wildly under the influence of alcohol; whereas B is struck by D, who, like B himself, has had his attention briefly distracted. When apportioning responsibility between A and C, by far the greater share will be attributed to C, so that A might lose no more than $10,000 of his assessment. B and D, on the other hand, would have the damages divided equally between them. Thus B loses $50,000, whereas A loses only $10,000, for similar behaviour. One has to be lucky in one's defendant! The anomalies multiply where more than one defendant is involved.

2.221 <u>Contribution between Tortfeasors.</u> Another legislative reform which came too late was the abolition of the common law rule prohibiting contribution between tortfeasors. If two cars collide, causing injury to a passenger, it might seem fair that each driver should contribute to the damages payable in proportion to his

24. See P S Atiyah, <u>Accidents, Compensation and the Law</u> (1970), 152-3.

responsibility. When, however, the damages are not
paid by the drivers themselves, but by their compulsory
insurers, litigation to determine the degrees of
responsibility is wasteful and unnecessary. Insurers
have long recognized this by entering into knock-for-
knock and claims-sharing agreements, which avoid the
costs of attributing fault. The courts have not yet
come to that realization. For instance, they are still
ready to interpret liberally legislation giving an
employer (in reality his insurer) a right to recover
workers' compensation he has paid, from a "wrongdoer"
(in practice only worthwhile if there is a liability
insurer behind him). Thus in Tickle Industries Pty Ltd
v Hann (1974) 48 ALJR 149, 151, Barwick CJ said:
"There is obvious and necessary justice in giving the
employer, who has been involved in the payment of
compensation by the wrongful act of another, a right of
recovery against that other .... It is also necessarily
just that the employee shall not be able to defeat that
right of recovery." The justness is not as obvious at
the beginning of the last quarter of the 20th century
as it must have been at the end of the 19th. It is to
the solution to all these problems presented by the
National Compensation Act that we now turn.

Chapter 3

THE NATIONAL COMPENSATION ACT

Sec 1:   REPLACEMENT OF PRESENT SYSTEMS

3.101   Abolition of Common Law Remedies.   The
National Compensation Act[1] provides for the payment of
a range of benefits for incapacity or death as a result
of personal injury or sickness.   These benefits are
discussed hereafter.   Section 97(1) states that it is
the intention of Parliament that such benefits are to
be in substitution for any damages recoverable in
respect of the injury, sickness or death for which they
are payable.   Accordingly, no action may be brought to
recover damages (s 97(3)).   The prohibition on recovering damages may not be avoided by refusing to lodge a
claim for benefits under the Act (s 97(2)).   If
constitutionally valid, this will effectively abolish
all common law actions for damages for personal injury
and death in Australia where benefits are payable under
the Act.   The only exception relates to claims for
death and injury in aeroplane accidents.   This exception stems from the implementation of Australia's
obligations under international conventions relating to
aircraft, such as the Warsaw Convention (see the Civil
Aviation (Carriers' Liability) Act 1959-73 and the

---

1.   See par 1.403 for the assumptions which are here
     made about the enactment of the National Compensa-
     tion Bill 1974.

Civil Aviation (Damage by Aircraft) Act 1958-73, the
operation of which is preserved by s 97(4)).

3.102   Overseas Actions.   The Australian Parliament
cannot, of course, abolish actions for damages in
jurisdictions outside Australia.   Thus an Australian
resident injured on a visit to, say, the United States
may have a claim for damages there, as well as being
entitled to benefits under the Act.   If he does receive
any benefit, he may be required to pay to Australia an
amount specified by the Secretary of the Department of
Repatriation and Compensation, not exceeding the amount
of the damages he has recovered (s 98).   This appears
to be the literal meaning of section 98(1) and would
place people injured abroad on a footing of equality
with people injured at home: all would effectively be
deprived of their rights to damages.   However, it is
possible that the intention is that the Secretary would
require repayment of the benefits paid under the Act,
rather than the damages recovered, since it is provided
(s 98(4)) that, after making such a requirement, the
Secretary shall forthwith cancel further payment of the
benefit concerned   (see Report, Vol 1, par 356(f)).
Furthermore, the constitutional validity of requiring
payment to Australia of damages recovered abroad is
much more doubtful than that of requiring repayment of
benefits.   Whether or not he would lose the fruits of
his action, a person injured abroad should hesitate
before suing, since loss of the benefits under the Act,
which could otherwise be payable for the rest of his
life, or until he reaches 65, may be a far more severe
penalty.

3.103   Deterrent to Damages Actions.   The provisions
of section 98 are not on their wording confined to
injuries occurring abroad, though that is the most
likely area of their application.   They would also

apply to an injury occurring within Australia, but
caused by a foreign person or company, who could
possibly be sued in his or its home jurisdiction.
Literally they would apply also to actions within
Australia if section 97(3) is held to be beyond the
powers of the Federal Parliament. If section 97(3) is
invalid, so that damages actions cannot be prevented,
it is unlikely that under section 98 the Secretary
could require payment over to Australia of the damages
recovered, but he may well be able to require repayment
of benefits already paid and to cancel further payment
of benefits. This should act as a deterrent to common
law actions.

   3.104 Surviving Common Law Actions. There is
nothing in the Act to prohibit actions at common law
where no benefits are payable under the Act. As some
benefits would always be payable on death where damages
are presently available, it seems that the various
State enactments of Lord Campbell's Act will generally
be redundant. A possible exception is that a claim by
a husband under Lord Campbell's Act for the loss of the
services of his wife would survive, since no benefits
are payable to widowers as such. On the other hand,
section 97(1) speaks in general terms of "a benefit in
respect of ... death," and since funeral benefits (s 46)
would always be payable, though not necessarily to the
widower, it may be that that will be regarded as
sufficient to oust the widower's claim. Furthermore,
section 96(a) makes it clear that claims for loss of
services are among those intended to be replaced by
benefits. Nevertheless, there are some instances of
personal injury actions which would certainly continue.
Under the Act benefits become payable only where an
injured person is "incapacitated". Although
"incapacity" is defined in very wide terms (s 4(1)),

including "the impairment of ... the well-being of [a]
person", not every incapacity in this sense entitles a
person to a benefit. Thus, for instance, an incapacity
lasting less than a week will in many instances not
give rise to a right to a benefit; nor will an
incapacity lasting less than three weeks in the case of
a non-earner; nor will a partial incapacity in the case
of a self-employed person, no matter how long it lasts
provided it is not permanent. In many of these
instances it would probably not be worth suing, but the
possibility remains.

3.105 Children. More serious is the survival of
common law actions in the case of injured children.
Benefits (except under s 50; see par 4.501) are not
payable to a person until he attains the "qualifying
age" (s 18(1)). That age is defined in section 4(1) as
the age of 18, or the age at which he first engages in
full-time employment, or first earns $50 per week as an
employee or self-employed person, whichever occurs
first. Thus a schoolchild, unless eligible for
benefits under section 50 to recompense him for
expenses, is not precluded from suing at common law, no
matter how serious the injury. Even though he would
otherwise become entitled to receive benefits in
respect of permanent incapacity, or temporary incapacity
extending beyond the qualifying age, once he attains
the qualifying age, section 17(2) requires him to sue
at common law and fail to recover damages before
becoming eligible for such benefits. If he recovers
any damages, however inadequate, he cannot claim
benefits in respect of his incapacity extending into
adulthood. Inadequacy may be due to an optimistic
assessment of his prospects of recovery, an under-
estimation of the loss he will sustain or a substantial
reduction for contributory negligence. Furthermore,

even though his damages may be assessed adequately, he
may actually recover no more than a small proportion of
his judgment, since compulsory insurance is abolished
by section 99. The denial of benefits under the Act in
such circumstances is obviously unjust and should be
amended.

3.106   Other objections to these provisions relating
to children may be put from the community's viewpoint.
The assessment of damages in the case of a seriously
injured young child is particularly difficult.[2]   Owing
to the possibility of liability to pay substantial
damages, potential defendants will need to maintain
insurance policies, though these will no longer be
compulsory (s 99). Although the premiums should be low
because the risk is a small one, considerable extra
administrative expenses will be incurred. (This
assumes that most people would not bother to insure
against the possibility of liability for the small
amounts payable in the cases referred to in par 3.104,
but would not want to risk their assets being taken in
satisfaction of the large judgment obtainable by a
seriously injured child.) Other unnecessary administrative expenses will be incurred in maintaining court
control over the lump-sum damages awarded until the
attainment of majority by the children, an exercise
which at present involves a large-scale operation.[3]
Finally, the requirement that before being eligible for
benefits in respect of incapacity extending beyond the
qualifying age, a child must exhaust his other remedies
may lead to the launching of hopeless common law
actions in order to provide the necessary proof.

---

2.   A recent example is <u>Rose</u> v <u>MVIT</u> (1974) 48 ALJR
     352.
3.   See the figures for the amounts invested, which
     were then already huge, in (1972) 46 ALJ 135.

3.107 Other Existing Remedies. Since "damages"
include compensation, "by whatever name called"
(s 4(1)), section 97 takes away the existing remedies
under workers' compensation legislation and no-fault
motor accident schemes. Should they survive on
constitutional grounds (see Chapter 6, Sec 1), the Act
by abolishing compulsory insurance (s 99), may deprive
them of some of their funds. However, the Report
contemplates that the statutes will all be repealed by
the appropriate legislatures. Presumably, the repeal
of even the workers' compensation acts and ordinances
governing Commonwealth employees and the Territories is
to await the actual coming into operation of the
National Compensation Scheme set up by the Act. Amendments to the social security legislation will also be
necessary to prevent overlap. The Report (Vol 1, par
345(d)) states, too, that less favourable repatriation
benefits should be merged in the new scheme. That
would no doubt have to await the outcome of the
independent inquiry into the whole question of
repatriation benefits which was set up under the former
Government and which has not yet reported.

Sec 2:   THE INTRODUCTION OF THE SCHEME

3.201 Personal Injury. Although the National
Compensation Scheme is designed ultimately to meet the
needs of all incapacitated Australians, whether their
incapacity is due to injury or sickness and whenever
that incapacity was caused, the Act makes provision for
the introduction in stages of the right to claim
benefits. The first stage will apply to persons
suffering personal injury after 1st July 1976 (s 19(a)
and the definition of "commencing date" in s 4(1)).
Thereafter, a date will be fixed by Proclamation

whereafter benefits will become payable in respect of
injuries occurring before 1st July 1976, though the
benefits themselves will not be paid retrospectively
(s 19(b)). Thus, assuming X is injured on 1st July
1975 and that the Proclamation fixes 1st July 1977 as
the date from which benefits become payable for
injuries occurring before 1st July 1976, then X will be
entitled to benefits from 1st July 1977, or the date
when he lodges his claim if that is later (s 19(b)(ii)).
Such benefits can only be in respect of X's continuing
incapacity after 30th June 1977; if he has fully
recovered by then, he cannot claim any benefits; nor
can he recover "back pay" for any permanent or continuing incapacity as it affected him before 1st July 1977.

    3.202 <u>Congenital Disability</u>. The <u>Report</u> recommended
that owing to the difficulty of distinguishing between
physical and mental defects in the newly born caused by
injury to the foetus or a parent's reproductive organs
and such defects due to natural causes, congenital
abnormalities should be included with injuries in the
first phase of the scheme, whatever their supposed
origin. This has been accepted: a physical or mental
defect, including a disease, occurring or existing at
or shortly after birth is to be treated as a personal
injury if it manifests itself before the age of 3
(s 9(e)). Therefore, if the mother caught rubella
during the early stages of pregnancy and the child
shows signs of deafness before the age of 3, the cost
of a hearing aid could be claimed under section 50.
When the child reaches the qualifying age, incapacity
benefits would become payable even if the sickness
scheme has not yet been introduced. On the other hand,
childhood illnesses are not covered under the injury
part of the scheme merely because they occur within the
first three years of life. A child that contracts

encephalitis at the age of 2 and is left mentally
retarded must await the commencement of the sickness
part of the scheme to be eligible for benefits. If the
defect can be traced to a sickness which is not
associated with the actual birth, no matter how
"shortly" afterwards it occurs, it would probably fall
outside the injury scheme. If there is no known cause,
then it can be assumed to be congenital and within the
first phase of the scheme.

3.203 As the congenitally disabled are included
among the injured, children born on or after 1st July
1976 with a physical or mental defect will be immediately within the scope of the scheme. Handicapped
children born before that date will have to await the
extension of the scheme by Proclamation to people
injured before that date. Of course, a neo-nate,
whenever born, may suffer an accidental injury and come
within the ordinary provisions of the first phase: cf
Smith v Browne [1974] VR 842; the administration of the
wrong eye-drops, causing blindness, would fall within
Part XIV of the Schedule, which sets out occurrences
giving rise to a "personal injury" under section 8(1).

3.204 Sickness. The sickness provisions of the
scheme, like those for personal injury, are to be
introduced in two stages. The first stage will come
into operation on a date fixed by Proclamation, which
date cannot be earlier than 1st July 1979 (s 21).
People suffering incapacity as a result of sickness
occurring after that date will then be covered. A
further Proclamation will thereafter apply the scheme
to people who, as a result of sickness which occurred
before the previously proclaimed date, are still
suffering incapacity.

3.205 Schematic Representation. The introduction of
the scheme may be represented as follows:

Time ———→

```
_____
           |        |                    |       |
           A        B                    C       D
```

A is 1st July 1976, from which date people injured or
  born congenitally disabled thereafter will be covered.

B is the date from which people injured or born congenitally disabled before A and still incapacitated will
  receive benefits.

C is the date, not earlier than 1st July 1979, from
  which people incapacitated by sickness occurring
  thereafter will be covered.

D is the date from which people who fell sick before C
  and who are still incapacitated will receive benefits.

Of course, the gaps between the dates, as represented
above, are not to scale. At the date of writing it is
not known when B, C and D will happen.

3.206 Death. The phasing-in of the benefits payable
on death corresponds to that in the case of incapacity
benefits. Where a person dies on or after 1st July
1976 as a result of injury, a pension becomes payable
to his widow under Part VI and funeral benefits and
children's and other relatives' benefits become payable
under Division 4 of Part V. Where the death occurred
before 1st July 1976 as a result of injury, the widow's
pension and children's benefits become payable - at
reduced rates (ss 58 and 47(3)) - from point B (as set
out in the previous par): sections 56(2)(a) and
47(4)(a). The widow and children will be entitled to
their benefits immediately after the death where that
occurs after point C as a result of sickness (ss 55(4)
and 45). Finally, from point D widows and children
will be entitled to their respective reduced pensions
and benefits even though the death occurred before
point C as a result of sickness (ss 56(2)(b) and

$47(4)(b)$). The benefit payable to other relatives
under section 48 and funeral benefit under section 46
apply only prospectively, ie in the case of death by
injury, after 1st July 1976; and in the case of death
as a result of sickness, after point C. Death as a
result of sickness must be taken throughout to include
death due to the ordinary process of ageing, since
"sickness" is defined as meaning "a physical or mental
disability, or physical or mental damage, that is not
personal injury" $(s\ 4(1))$.

3.207 Justification for Phasing. Once we reach
point D in time (as set out in par 3.205) the needs of
all Australians, with rare exceptions, will be met in
the same way, whether those needs were created by
negligence, natural disaster or nephritis. Why should
we not move immediately to this stage? The Report did
not itself recommend the four-stage introduction which
was adopted by the Act, but suggested that there could
be two stages: first for injury and congenital
disability and then for sickness. The main reason for
this was, as shown in the committee's terms of reference, that the Government was committed to a personal
injury scheme, but not necessarily to one covering
sickness. The Government could see how the injury
scheme works in practice before making a final decision
on sickness. Significant, too, is the costing of the
schemes. On the committee's estimates, the entire cost
of the personal injury scheme, including congenital
disabilities, could be met for less than is spent at
present on compulsory motor vehicle and workers'
compensation schemes (see pars 6.202-4). All that is
required is a diversion of funds from one direction to
another. The sickness scheme, on the other hand,
requires the raising of a fairly large amount of extra
revenue (see par 6.209). The community will have to

decide whether it can afford it.

3.208   As mentioned in the previous paragraph, the
committee did not subdivide the two phases of its
proposed scheme. Its cost estimates were based on a
"plateau" after the scheme had notionally been in force
many years. Since its conclusion was that payment to
people retrospectively injured did not increase the
costs beyond the total of existing schemes, it saw no
reason to exclude them from the immediate operation of
the scheme. The Government, however, probably foresaw
administrative difficulty in coping at the same time
with all past injuries and those occurring in the
future; it accordingly decided to allow the administrative procedures to become smoothly established before
bringing in retrospective cases.

Sec 3:   THE DEFINITION OF PERSONAL INJURY

3.301   Necessity For. Once the National Compensation
Scheme is fully operative (ie when point D in par 3.205
is reached) there will generally be no need to
distinguish between the causes of incapacity or death.
However, for as long as the phasing-in process lasts a
distinction will have to be made between those
incapacities which are due to personal injury and those
due to other causes. Even after point D is reached it
will be necessary to make the distinction in a few
instances, since the injury part of the scheme will
apply to visitors to Australia, but the sickness part
will not (s 23). Also, the waiting-period for the
commencement of injury benefits will be shorter than
that for the commencement of sickness benefits
(s 24(1)(a)). This problem has plagued the New Zealand
scheme, where only personal injury is covered and the
appropriate definition is still unsettled.

3.302 <u>The Schedule</u>. The solution adopted by the committee was to treat as personal injury incapacities due to external causes as classified in <u>The International Classification of Diseases</u> issued by the World Health Organization. The relevant categories, E800 to E999, ranging from railway accidents - through poisoning, falls, accidents due to natural and environmental factors and many others - to injury resulting from operations of war, are reproduced in the Schedule to the Act. The only category excluded is E978, which refers to legal execution, since section 14 specifically removes death by judicial execution from the scope of the Act. The committee considered this classification as exhaustive and appropriate, but contemplated the possible amendment of the Schedule by addition or deletion, should unforeseen cases occur.

3.303 <u>Definition</u>. Section 8(1) therefore provides the basic definition of "personal injury" as meaning "a physical or mental injury or other physical or mental damage or effect that is caused by an occurrence specified in, or is caused in circumstances specified in, the Schedule". Subsequent sections amplify the definition and in one instance reduce its possible scope. Paragraphs (a) and (b) of section 9 bring within the definition mental or nervous shock and psychiatric illness caused by or in occurrences or circumstances specified in the Schedule; and paragraphs (c) and (d) thereof ensure that industrial diseases and "boilermaker's deafness" are encompassed. As previously mentioned (par 3.202) congenital disabilities are also treated as personal injury, however caused (s 9(e)). The "contracting, acceleration, aggravation, exacerbation or deterioration of a disease as a result of personal injury is also personal injury" for the purposes of the Act (s 11).

3.304   Medical Misadventures. Although Part XIV of
the Schedule lists "Surgical and Medical Complications
and Misadventures", section 10 specifically provides
that "a misadventure in connexion with medical,
surgical, dental or first-aid treatment, care or
attention of a person is also personal injury". This
specific provision does not limit in any way the list
in the Schedule (s 8(2)), but may extend it. No doubt
there will be particular difficulties here in distinguishing a "misadventure" from a mere failure to cure.
Unquestionably, an unusual allergic reaction to medical
treatment will be covered, whether due to negligence on
the part of the doctor or not. So if the facts of
Robinson v Post Office [1974] 2 All ER 737 (CA) were to
recur in Australia the reaction to the tetanus vaccine
would be classified under item 119 of the Schedule and
the detailed investigation of whether the doctor was at
fault would be avoided. But it might still be
necessary in some cases, in order to determine whether
there has been a "misadventure", to ask whether there
were some procedures which the doctor could have
adopted to prevent the normal development of the
disease from which the patient was suffering when he
consulted a medical practitioner.

3.305   Heart Attacks and Cancer. One of the most
fruitful sources of litigation with regard to workers'
compensation has been connected with heart attacks
suffered at work. Once the Australian statutes were
amended to allow compensation for injuries occurring
in the course of, though not necessarily arising out
of, the employment, a good deal of effort was expended
to show that various stages in the development of
coronary disease were themselves "injuries" if they

occurred at work. [1] The Act makes it clear that cardiac
episodes, and malignant neoplasms, are not, without
more, to be treated as personal injury (s 12).
Accepting, however, that the exclusion of all heart and
cancerous conditions would deprive workers of rights
under existing legislation, the Act covers as personal
injury cardiac episodes and malignant neoplasms
contributed to or aggravated by employment. Much
litigation has also been generated by similar workers'
compensation provisions, but disputes are presumably
unavoidable until the general sickness provisions come
into operation. Although heart attacks and cancers
occurring away from the place of employment are covered
if contributed to by the employment, there is no
provision for cardiac episodes or malignant neoplasms
contributed to by travelling to or from work.
Furthermore, since section 12 takes precedence over the
Schedule (s 8(3)), heart attacks precipitated by railway, motor or other accidents, if not in the course of
the sufferer's employment, are excluded until all sickness comes within the scope of the scheme.

Sec 4:   COVERAGE AS TO PERSONS

3.401 <u>Australian Residents</u>. Persons whose usual
place of residence is in Australia will be covered in
respect of personal injury (s 16(1)) and sickness
(s 20) suffered by them in Australia. They will also
be covered in respect of injury and sickness outside
Australia if it occurred within one year after they
last left Australia (ss 16(5) and 20).

---

1. See generally the writer's article in (1966) 40
    ALJ 179 and the references there cited.

3.402 <u>Other Australians Abroad</u>. The one year time-
limit (s 16(5)) does not apply to certain Australians
who might normally be expected to be overseas for
longer periods. These are members of the Defence Force
and former Australian residents overseas in connexion
with their employment or studies, provided the latter
intended to return when their duties or studies were
completed (s 16(2)). The spouse and certain close
relatives (s 16(3)) of a person so qualified are also
included. If one of these persons ceases to be
qualified - eg a member of the Defence Force resigns or
a student gives up his studies - he continues to be
covered abroad for one year.

3.403 <u>Visitors</u>. Non-residents of Australia are
covered against personal injury, but not sickness,
suffered in Australia (ss 16(1) and 23). However, they
would not be covered even against personal injury if it
occurred on a ship or aeroplane above the continental
shelf of Australia unless the ship or aeroplane is
registered in Australia or its operations are based on
a place in Australia (s 15(1)). (It is not clear why
s 15(1) refers to "sickness" as well as personal injury,
since non-residents are in any event excluded from
sickness benefits and the subsection, by virtue of
s 15(2), does not apply to Australian residents and the
people referred to in par 3.402.)

3.404 <u>Criminals</u>. Persons injured during the
commission of certain crimes, for which they are
subsequently convicted, are not entitled to benefits
under the scheme (s 13). The list of crimes specified
is brief: it comprises murder; intentionally causing
grievous bodily harm; piracy; an act done with the
intention of endangering a person on board a vehicle,
vessel or aircraft; revolt against the authority of the
captain of a ship or aircraft; and attempts at these

crimes. Unlike the view of the common law taken by the
High Court in Smith v Jenkins (1970) 119 CLR 397, there
is not seen to be any public policy against compensa-
ting people injured while committing such offences as
the illegal use of a motor car. After all, such people
are often the victims of social pressures created in
consequence of the community's inadequate provision of
recreational facilities and the deification of the motor
car. The criminal law exists to punish them and there
is no need to add to their penalty by depriving them of
rights to compensation. Their dependants, too, are
often completely innocent. Where a person has been
imprisoned, and is thus already being kept at State
expense, the Secretary may suspend, postpone or cancel
the whole or part of any benefit payable, or pay it
instead, in whole or part, to a dependant of the
beneficiary (s 115). Where the injury occurs while a
person is imprisoned, benefit is not payable in respect
of incapacity during the period of imprisonment
(s 115(2)). The dependants of a person judicially
executed are also not entitled to death benefits (s 14).

3.405 Self-injurers. Workers' compensation legislation generally excludes injuries which are wilfully
self-inflicted. The Act contains no similar exclusion.
The committee accepted evidence of psychiatrists
(Report, Vol 1, par 351(a)) that the incidence of
suicide is not likely to be increased because dependants
would be compensated. It also regarded deliberate
self-injury as a manifestation of some form of mental
illness: "whatever may have been the muddled motive or
emotion, the condition itself will have created a need
that should be met" (ibid, par 351(b)).

3.406 Children. Attention has already been drawn
(par 3.105) to the fact that benefits, other than those
under section 50, are not payable to children until
they reach the age of 18, or first engage in full-time
employment or earn $50 per week (s 18). This provision
has been the subject of justifiable criticism on a
number of grounds. There seems no good reason why a
newsboy whose incapacity may persist for a number of
years, but not extend beyond the qualifying age, should
not be compensated at all for his loss of earnings
unless he is able to sue at common law. In many
families children would be expected to start contribu-
ting to the family income from the age of 16 and it is
unfair that children permanently incapacitated while
very young should have to wait until 18 to start
receiving benefits. Even when a child who is injured
when less than 15 reaches the qualifying age, since his
earnings in the year preceding his injury could not
have exceeded $50 per week, the absolute limit to the
benefit payable to him will be $42.50 (s 33(3)),
subject only to increase by reason of inflation (see
par 4.704; cf for a child over 15, s 29 (par 4.215)).

3.407 The Aged. Benefits under the Act generally
cease to be payable at the age of 65 (s 18(2)). The
Report (Vol 1, par 355(d)) contemplated the possible
need for the adjustment of this provision "depending
upon the outcome of the present inquiry into a superannuation scheme for Australia". It assumed that a
national superannuation scheme would come into existence
and recommended that compensation benefits should cut
out where the superannuation scheme took over. Since,
however, any national superannuation scheme is still a
long way from implementation, the Act should meanwhile
be amended to provide for compensation benefits in

cases where earnings would probably have continued
beyond the age of 65.

  3.408 Although under the Act in its present form
benefits generally cease to be payable at the age of
65, it is not true to say that people over 65 are not
covered by the scheme. Under section 18(2), if any
person over 61 is injured, benefits may continue for up
to four years. Thus, whether a person is 61, 65, 71 or
101 when he is injured, he would receive compensation
for four years should he live so long and his incapacity
be declared permanent. Also where a husband dies, it
does not matter at what age the death occurs: the
widow will be eligible for the pension until she
attains the age of 65 (s 56(3)). So, too, the various
death benefits payable under Division 4 of Part V are
not dependent on the death occurring before the age of
65.

Chapter 4

BENEFITS UNDER THE ACT

Sec 1: GENERALLY

4.101 <u>Payable Weekly</u>. The Act provides that, apart
from a few exceptional instances, benefits are payable
in weekly instalments (s 100). If the relevant period
for payment of a benefit is less than a week, then a
proportionate amount is payable (s 100(2)). One
exception relates to disfigurement, in which case a
lump sum of up to $10,000 may be awarded (s 51).
Another exception concerns widows: they receive a lump
sum of $1,000 on the death of their husbands and, in
some instances, a further lump sum if they remarry
while in receipt of a pension (s 57). Medical expenses
and costs of appliances and assistance, and funeral
expenses, will also be reimbursed by way of lump sums
(ss 50 and 46).

4.102 <u>Commutation</u>. The <u>Report</u> rightly[1] adopted the
philosophy that only in limited circumstances should

---

1. For a detailed criticism of the common law
    requirement that damages be awarded by way of a
    lump sum, see H Luntz, <u>The Assessment of Damages
    for Personal Injury and Death</u> (1974), 16-9.
    Despite the lack of enthusiasm detected by the Law
    Commission in England (<u>Report on Assessment of
    Damages</u>, LC 56, 1973, pars 26-30), the present
    writer adheres to his advocacy of weekly payments,
    even though it may smack of paternalism. The
    State, which would in any event have to assume the
    care of a person who dissipated a lump sum intended

beneficiaries be able to cbtain a lump sum in commuta-
tion of future weekly payments. This philosophy is
given effect to in section 54. Benefits payable for an
incapacity which has been determined to be or is likely
to become total, whether temporary or permanent, may
never be commuted. Nor may benefits for temporary
partial incapacity or benefits payable to a child be
commuted. Widows' pensions, being dealt with in a part
of the Act other than Part V, also fall outside the
application of section 54. Other benefits - mainly
relating to permanent partial disability - may be
converted into a lump sum in some circumstances. If
the value of the lump sum, calculated by discounting
the weekly payments until the age of 65 (or for four
years where the injury occurs after 61) at a rate of
interest to be prescribed, is up to $3,000, it may be
obtained as of right by the beneficiary. If the value
of the lump sum, as so calculated, exceeds $3,000, then
it is payable only if it is determined that (a) the
incapacity is not likely to become total; (b) the
beneficiary intends to use the capital in a manner
particularly advantageous to him; and (c) in all the
circumstances, it is desirable in his interests that
the benefit should be paid by way of a lump sum.

    4.103   Thus in those cases where rehabilitation is
likely to be assisted by taking the beneficiary off
weekly payments - mostly instances of "compensation

---

        to provide for his future needs, is entitled to
        guard itself against the immature judgment of its
        citizens who overestimate the value of an immediate
        award as against long-term benefits. This is
        particularly so as inflation becomes more and more
        uncontrollable. The Law Commission's recommenda-
        tion that periodic payments should not be
        introduced was confined to a fault-based system,
        whatever merits they might have within a different
        system of compensation for injury (par 29).

neurosis" - the Secretary may award a lump sum if he is
satisfied that the incapacity is not likely to become
total and that the beneficiary has a sound avenue for
the investment of the lump sum, eg the purchase of a
block of flats or successful small business. It is
noteworthy that although the lump sum is to be
calculated by discounting the weekly payments, no
deduction is to be made for "contingencies" or the
"vicissitudes of life" as is done at common law. Even
the death of the beneficiary before the age of 65 is
not to be allowed for. For this reason, but depending
on whether the rate of interest prescribed is low
enough to cope with the problem of inflation, the value
of the lump sum could well exceed the true actuarial
value of the weekly payments.

4.104 Benefits Inalienable. A beneficiary may not
assign the benefits to which he is entitled under the
Act (s 113). Nor are his rights capable of being taken
in execution by his creditors and they would not fall
into his bankrupt estate (ibid).

4.105 Lack of Capacity of Beneficiary. Sections 114
and 115 provide for payment in some circumstances to be
made to persons other than the beneficiary. While not
expressly so confined, the main application of these
sections would be to instances where the beneficiary is
suffering from a lack of capacity properly to handle
his own affairs, such as being under-age, mentally
deficient, hospitalized or imprisoned. Such lack of
capacity may be connected or entirely unconnected with
the incapacity which gives rise to the right to
benefits. Where payment is made to someone on behalf
of a beneficiary who has not attained the qualifying
age, that other person is required to apply the money
for the maintenance, training or advancement of the

beneficiary (s 114(2)). In other instances the money
can obviously be used for the support of the beneficiary's dependants.

4.106   Suspension and Cancellation.   Where a
beneficiary is imprisoned or hospitalized or refuses to
co-operate in ways specified, payment may be suspended,
postponed or cancelled (ss 115 and 117).   Imprisonment
has already been dealt with (par 3.404).   Where the
beneficiary is an inmate of a hospital, nursing home or
benevolent institution, in deciding whether to suspend,
postpone or cancel payment of the benefit the Secretary
is required to take into account all the circumstances,
including the extent of hospital benefits payable under
legislation, such as the National Health Act, and
whether charges at the institution are reduced by
reason of State grants (s 115(3)).   Non-co-operation
which could lead to the suspension, postponement or
cancellation of benefits consists in failing to furnish
medical certificates as required, failing to submit to
medical examination by a specified medical practitioner
or failure to take steps regarded by the Secretary as
reasonable for the beneficiary's rehabilitation (s 117).
No doubt these measures are necessary to deal with
malingerers, and some cases of genuine psychological
overlay, but it is to be hoped that they will be
sparingly exercised.   There is also a general provision
permitting the cancellation, suspension or reduction of
a benefit where

> "(a)   having regard to the provisions of this Act
> and to any information in the possession of, or to
> any circumstances known to, the Secretary; or (b)
> by reason of the failure or omission of a benefic-
> iary to comply with a provision of this Act, the
> Secretary considers that a benefit should be
> cancelled or suspended or that the rate of a
> benefit is greater or less than it should be"
> (s 104(1)).

Despite its extremely wide language this provision is
no doubt intended to apply only to cases such as where
the beneficiary has provided false information as to
his earnings or a fraudulent medical certificate.
Before any decision adverse to him may be made, a
beneficiary must be informed in writing of the proposed
decision (s 105(1)). He may then ask for the matter to
be reconsidered and must be given the opportunity of
being heard. If an adverse decision is then forthcoming, the beneficiary may appeal (s 105(2)).

4.107 <u>Benefits Unpaid at Death</u>. Under section 118,
where a benefit had accrued due to a beneficiary but
had not yet been paid to him at his death, the
Secretary may, on application, pay it to the person
whom the Secretary determines is best entitled to
receive it. The same applies in respect of a claim not
yet processed when the applicant dies. These payments
are to be distinguished from the sums which become payable to dependants of the beneficiary in their own
right on his death (ss 57, 47 and 48). Application for
the posthumous amounts due to the deceased beneficiary
must be made within six months of his death, or such
extended period as the Secretary allows. The Secretary
has a complete discretion whether to pay the amount to
the deceased's executor or other personal representative
or to a dependant or other person.

Sec 2:   TOTAL INCAPACITY

4.201 <u>Meaning</u>. Section 40 prescribes that benefits
are payable for "total incapacity". No attempt is made
in the Act to define total incapacity. "Incapacity"
alone is defined, "in relation to a person", as meaning
"the impairment of - (a) the ability of that person to
engage in work that is useful or gainful; or (b) the

well-being of that person, or both". It is difficult
to imagine anything wider than that encompassed by (b)
and one might wonder why (a) is necessary unless it is
designed to show that every headache or cold is <u>not</u> to
be taken as "incapacity" because it impairs the "well-
being" of a person. What incapacity is to be regarded
as "total" is left by section 40 to the determination
of the Secretary. Except when a person is dead, or a
"living vegetable", it would be hard to say that his
well-being had been totally impaired, so that here,
where the definition of "incapacity" has to be used
negatively, part (a) of the definition can be expected
to offer more guidance. Nevertheless, if the Secretary
were to require a total inability to engage in work
that is useful or gainful, there would still be very
few cases of total incapacity indeed. Even quadriplegics are often capable of useful work. Furthermore,
since the benefits for total incapacity are clearly
intended to provide the earnings-related compensation
which is the key-stone of the scheme, the whole
structure would collapse if people incapacitated for,
say, three or four weeks from performing their normal
work were treated as not totally incapacitated because
they were still capable of looking after their gardens
or doing other domestic chores.

4.202 Some help with this conundrum is furnished by
section 35(3). In cases of permanent partial incapacity
a medical practitioner is required to certify in
writing the percentage of incapacity (s 35(1)). The
method of ascertaining the percentage is prescribed in
section 35(4) (see par 4.304). Section 35(3) provides:
"Where the percentage specified in the certificate is
85 or more, the person shall be taken to be totally
incapacitated."

4.203 Nevertheless, this is not a solution to the problem. Eighty-five per cent incapacity requires a very severe degree of impairment indeed. A person who has suffered brain damage so that he cannot comprehend language symbols, but can himself produce unintelligible language, falls within the range of 50-85 per cent. The amputation of a whole arm constitutes only 70 per cent incapacity and of a whole leg only 50 per cent (see Table, par 4.304). Mere immobilization of limbs in plaster, not being permanent, would not even come within the Guides. Yet it would be quite unrealistic to expect a person temporarily disabled from carrying on his normal occupation by, say, a fractured leg to train for some other occupation for which he is capable when he will be perfectly able to resume his ordinary work once the plaster is removed. Where the convalescence is prolonged it may be reasonable to expect a person unable meanwhile to engage in his normal work to attempt some other employment for which he is fitted, if it is available, and thus not to treat him as "totally incapacitated" throughout the period. But in the immediate aftermath of an accident, it would be unfair not to treat a person as totally incapacitated merely because theoretically he is fit to engage in work that is useful or gainful. For self-employed people it is particularly important that "total incapacity" should not be narrowly construed, since in their case there are not available benefits for temporary partial incapacity (see par 4.303).

4.204 It is therefore submitted that the Act ought to be amended to require the Secretary, in determining whether a person is "totally incapacitated", to have regard (a) to the occupation, if any, of that person before he was incapacitated; and (b) where he was gainfully employed, to the reasonable availability of gainful work for which that person is fitted during the period of incapacity. Then, in the case of a housewife, she would be treated as totally incapacitated if she was incapable of performing all or most of her domestic activities; if she could still do many, she would be partially incapacitated. In the case of an earner, he would be treated as totally incapacitated if he was unable to be employed in the job he ordinarily engaged in and either it was not reasonable to expect him to find another job or such other job was not reasonably available to him.

4.205 Commencement of Benefits. Subject to the exceptions in paragraphs 4.207-9 benefits for total incapacity resulting from injury will commence to be payable on the eighth day after a person became incapacitated (s 41(1)(a)). The benefits will not then be retrospective. It was thought desirable to shift the cost of the first week's incapacity entirely to the injured or their employers under normal sick-pay agreements (Report, Vol 1, par 377). One reason was to filter out the very large number of minor injuries which would otherwise press down on the fund and its administrative processes. This could have been achieved simply by making a person ineligible for benefits unless the incapacity lasted more than a week, but if it did persist for that period allowing the benefits to be payable retrospectively. However, there were other reasons: employers would be relieved, at public expense, of already widespread sick-pay arrangements; criticism might be directed at the removal of personal initiatives to overcome small troubles; and there would be a heavy financial burden on a scheme designed for more pressing claims.

4.206 In the case of sickness the waiting period is
extended to three weeks (s 24(1)(a)). However, for
earners this waiting period serves mainly as a filter
for minor claims, since if the incapacity persists for
the requisite period benefits at the rate of $42.50 per
week (adjusted for inflation under s 95) will be payable
for the last two of those three weeks (s 24(2), where
the reference to "s 24(1)(b)" must be taken as a
misprint for "s 24(1)(a)": see <u>Report</u>, Vol 1, par
377(f)).

4.207 In the case of a person who did not earn any
money as an employee or self-employed person during the
period of four weeks immediately before his incapacity
commenced, no benefits at all are payable in respect of
incapacity during the first three weeks (s 43(1)).
Although it is justifiable to deny for a short period
- such as three weeks - a benefit based on notional
earnings to a person who was not earning at all in the
previous four weeks, this recommendation of the
committee, adopted in the Act, has the effect of deny-
ing also to such people recovery of expenses and losses
which they may incur during the period (see par 4.501).
Thus a housewife who has to employ domestic help during
a period of temporary total incapacity cannot recoup
the payments she has to make. A departure from the
committee's recommendation would here have been
desirable.

4.208 On the other hand section 43(2) introduces an
undesirable departure from the recommendations of the
committee. Yielding to trade union pressure the
Government has here provided that benefits shall
commence immediately, without the seven-day waiting
period, in cases where workers' compensation would have
been payable. This is undesirable for many reasons.
First, it reintroduces distinctions between people

according to circumstances which are purely fortuitous
and between residents of different States (cf par
2.108). Secondly, the determination of whether the
appropriate circumstances are satisfied could lead to
disputes, adversary proceedings before the appeal
tribunal and litigation in the courts. Thirdly, it
will clutter up the administrative processes with many
minor claims and so delay the desired speedy assessment
of more serious ones. Fourthly, it will increase the
cost of the scheme enormously and possibly make it
politically unacceptable. Finally, it is by no means
clear how one will determine when "compensation would
have been payable to an incapacitated person under the
law of a State or Territory or of another country,
being a law relating to compensation in respect of
illness suffered by employees" once all the workers'
compensation legislation has been repealed. It is
hardly to be expected that these acts will remain on
the statute books for this sole purpose. Apart from
all these reasons for not discriminating in favour of
workers, the pressure from the unions was really
unnecessary: it could have been much better directed
at employers to ensure that full sick-pay is made
available to all workers for up to one week, if not
more, where that is not already done.

4.209 There is no waiting period where a person in
receipt of a benefit suffers a further injury or sickness. If the incapacity from the second injury lasts
beyond the time when the benefit for the first would
normally have ceased, the benefit in respect of the
incapacity from the second injury commences immediately
the first benefit ceases (s 52).

4.210   Short-term Rate. For the first four weeks
that an incapacity continues after benefits begin to be
payable, the rate of benefit is at what may be called
the "short-term" rate (s 41(1)(a)). Thus in the case
of a person injured in circumstances where he was
previously entitled to workers' compensation, the
short-term rate will be payable from the date of injury
for up to four weeks. In the case of an earner injured
in other circumstances, if the incapacity continues for
five weeks or more, the short-term rate will be paid
from the eighth day to the end of the fifth week. In
the case of injury to a non-earner or sickness suffered
by anyone, the benefits will start after three weeks
and be payable at the short-term rate for four weeks
thereafter, if the incapacity continues so long. That
rate is ordinarily 85 per cent of the average earnings
of the person concerned, whether as an employee or
self-employed person, during the four weeks immediately
before his incapacity commenced (s 27). If for some
reason the average of his earnings during that period
does not fairly represent his average earnings, then
the average over another period, commencing not more
than five years previously, may be used by the Secretary
in determining the appropriate rate (s 30). If the
average is $500 or more, or $50 or less, per week then
the benefits will be $425 and $42.50 respectively
(s 31). The maximum and minimum will be automatically
adjusted each year in line with increases in average
weekly earnings (s 95). The provisions relating to
increases in the earnings of young persons (s 29; see
par 4.215) are also theoretically applicable to the
short-term rate, but are not likely to be of much
practical importance here. A person who was not
earning, such as a housewife, will receive the minimum,
ie $42.50, as adjusted annually.

4.211 "Earnings". In the case of an employee there
is a special definition of "earnings" (s 4(1)), which
will be applicable in the calculation of the benefits
at both the short-term and the long-term rates. It
"includes any of the following received or derived in
the capacity of employee:-

    (a)   wages, salaries, commissions and emoluments;
    (b)   bonuses, gratuities and honoraria;
    (c)   fees, including directors' fees;
    (d)   allowances, not being allowances in respect
         of expenses; and
    (e)   income from property, where that income is an
         emolument of employment or office".

Leave pay is also included (s 4(4)). However, specifically excluded are lump-sum payments on retirement or
retrenchment ("golden handshakes" and redundancy
payments); pension and superannuation payments; and
"the value of a benefit not received in the form of
money". This last exclusion has been rightly criticized
by the unions, since there seems to be no good reason
why an employee, particularly a farm-worker, who
receives part of the reward for his labour by way of
free or subsidized accommodation or food should not be
compensated for the loss of these benefits if he
becomes totally incapacitated. It would not be too
difficult to place a money value on these benefits.

4.212 Long-term Rate. If the incapacity persists
beyond four weeks, then the long-term rate becomes
payable (s 41(1)(b)). It is clear that this will apply
to injury from five weeks before point B is reached and
to sickness from seven weeks before point D is reached
(ss 41(1)(b) and 24(1)(b); for the meaning of "point B"
and "point D", see par 3.205). However, on the literal
wording of the Act, it seems that in the case of people
injured between point A and five weeks before point B,
once short-term benefits cut out, only $42.50 per week
will be payable until point B, whereafter long-term

benefits become payable (s 41(1)(b)(ii) and (2)).
Similar transitional provisions apply to sickness
(s 24(1)(b)). There is nothing in the Report which
explains or justifies the reduction in benefits until
the scheme becomes retrospectively operational.

4.213 The long-term rate will normally be 85 per
cent of the average earnings of the person concerned
during the year ending 30th June immediately preceding
the commencement of his incapacity, plus an allowance
for inflation between that 30th June and the beginning
of the quarter in which he was injured (s 28). The
average earnings of self-employed people may in
appropriate cases be ascertained over a period of three
years, instead of the ordinary one year (s 28(2) and
(3)). The adjustment for inflation is to be done in
accordance with a formula (s 28(5) and (6)). For
example, if average weekly earnings for the quarter
ending on the previous 30th June were $150 and for the
last quarter before the person was injured were $200,
then the average earnings of the person are to be
increased by $33\frac{1}{3}$ per cent for the purpose of calculating
his long-term benefits. Once the initial rate of
benefit is calculated, we are no longer concerned with
average earnings; future adjustments for inflation are
made in accordance with section 94 (see par 4.703).

4.214 In the case of long-term benefits, too, if the
average earnings over the previous year or three years
do not fairly represent the average earnings of the
person concerned, the Secretary may use another
appropriate period (s 30). The maximum is again 85 per
cent of $500 and for non-earners the benefit will be
$42.50 (s 31). This maximum and minimum will be
automatically adjusted for inflation (s 95). A
different minimum is to be laid down for full-time
employees (s 42). Here the Minister will from time to

time publish   a minimum wage and the benefit payable
will be at least that minimum or 100 per cent of the
employee's earnings, whichever is lower (s 42(3) and
(4)). Thus if the minimum specified by the Minister is
$100 and the average earnings of the employee were $110
per week, the benefit will be $100, not 85 per cent of
$110 ($93.50). If, in such case, the average earnings
of the employee were $90 per week, the benefit will be
$90 per week.

4.215 Future Earnings. In only a limited range of
cases are "future earnings" relevant to the assessment
of the benefits payable for total incapacity. Two
requirements must be satisfied before there may be
taken into account increases in earnings which an
incapacitated person might have expected to receive due
to promotion or other advancement: first, his usual
place of residence at the time when his incapacity
began must be in Australia; and, secondly, he must have
then been over 15 and under 31. If these criteria are
satisfied, then his weekly income may be adjusted at
the ages of 21, 26 and 31 to represent what it would
have been if he had not been incapacitated (s 29).
Where a person was a full-time student when he was
injured or fell sick, he will, if over 18, receive
benefits at the minimum rate until such time as his
full-time education would normally have been completed
(s 41(3)) and thereafter presumably at the rate
appropriate for what he would have earned, with adjustments at the ages of 21, 26 and 31.

4.216 The cut-off age of 31, after which future
earnings must be ignored, is rather arbitrary. Although
it is already an extension on the age of 26 suggested
in the Report, it can hardly be regarded as completely
satisfactory. This is particularly so in the case of
housewives. Some women with young families may be

ready to resume careers for which they were trained by
the age of 31; others who had their children in their
middle to late twenties may not have planned to do so
until a few years after that age. It is unfair that
the former should be entitled to have their earnings
from their possible careers taken into account, whereas
the latter will receive only the minimum rate for
permanent total incapacity. On the other hand, one can
see that in order to avoid contentious disputes, some
fairly early cut-off date must be selected: there
should be no encouragement of argument whether a rising
young barrister would have become a QC or even a judge,
whether a lecturer would have become a professor,
whether a doctor would have become an eminent surgeon
or other specialist. It should be enough to ensure
that, whatever the circumstances of his injury or sickness, he is able to maintain the standard of living
which he had already attained by virtue of his earnings.
In the interests of such certainty, members of the
community should be willing to forgo the possibility of
compensation which the common law now offers in some
cases for the loss of the chance of increased future
earnings.

4.217 Temporary or Permanent. Benefits for temporary
total incapacity, whether at the short-term or long-
term rate, naturally terminate when the incapacity
ceases to be total. Thus section 41(1) provides for
payment of these benefits only while the incapacity
continues. If the total incapacity becomes partial,
benefits for partial incapacity then become payable
(s 53(2)). However, once it is determined that the
incapacity is permanent, the benefits may not thereafter
be stopped merely because the beneficiary recovers and
is in fact able to employ himself gainfully (s 104(2)).
This provision is essential if rehabilitation is to be

encouraged. Yet there is nothing in the Act requiring
the Secretary to make a determination that an incapacity
is permanent within any specified time: the only
remedy would be an appeal against a refusal to make
such a determination (s 105). In many instances it
will be impossible to make such a determination quickly
owing to an uncertain medical prognosis; here resources
such as the provision of assistance from social workers
and other rehabilitative personnel will need to be
employed to prevent the development of anxiety neuroses.

Sec 3: PARTIAL INCAPACITY

4.301 Meaning. The definition of "incapacity", as
has already been pointed out (par 4.201), is extremely
broad: any impairment of the ability of a person to
engage in work that is useful or gainful or of his
well-being constitutes an "incapacity" (s 4(1)).
However, not every incapacity entitles a person to
benefits for partial incapacity. Thus no benefit is
payable if the incapacity is temporary and is determined
by the Secretary to be "insignificant" (s 39(2)). Even
if the incapacity is permanent, where the degree of
impairment (as ascertained in the manner described in
par 4.304) is 10 per cent or less, "the person shall
be taken not to be incapacitated", though certain lump
sums may then be payable (s 35(2); see par 4.306).

4.302 Temporary. If the incapacity is temporary,
but not insignificant, a benefit may be payable to a
person who was an employee at the time when his
incapacity commenced (s 39). The amount of the benefit
is left completely to the discretion of the Secretary,
up to a maximum of half the employee's average weekly
earnings as determined for the purposes of the "short-
term rate" (see par 4.210). The benefit is payable

only so long as the incapacity continues and will in any event terminate after 26 weeks unless the Secretary determines that it should continue for a further period not exceeding one year. The purpose of this benefit is to encourage rehabilitation, since it enables an employee to return to light work knowing that a drop in his wages can be compensated for by payment of up to half his previous earnings (Report, Vol 1, par 375).

4.303 No benefit for temporary partial disability is payable to self-employed and unemployed people. In the case of the former the Report states that "self-employed persons are usually able to organize some suitable work for themselves" (Vol 1, par 375(b)). This is unexceptionable in the context of the purpose for which the benefit for temporary partial incapacity was recommended, viz the encouragement of light work for rehabilitative purposes. However, people who suffer a temporary partial incapacity may incur expenses by reason of that incapacity for which they should be compensated. The section providing generally for reimbursement of expenses (s 50) does not apply, except in the case of children, unless some other benefit is payable. Thus nothing at all is payable to a self-employed chemist who, as a result of a broken arm, is unable to dispense, though he can still otherwise attend to his business. The Act should be amended to enable the chemist to recover the cost of employing a qualified dispenser. Similarly, it should be amended to allow an injured housewife to recover the cost of domestic assistance required because of her temporary partial incapacity. Furthermore, section 39 itself should be extended to members of the workforce who were temporarily unemployed at the time of their injury: such people, perhaps more than any others, need to be

encouraged to take light work for which they are fit
and which is available.

4.304   Permanent.   Where an incapacity is, or is
likely to be, permanent, its degree has to be assessed
by a medical practitioner, who is required to certify
in writing the percentage of the person's incapacity
(s 35(1)).   In arriving at the percentage the medical
practitioner must "have regard to" tables published by
an expert committee of the American Medical Association,
after years of work on the subject, in a book called
Guides to the Evaluation of Permanent Impairment
(s 35(4)).   An example of a comparatively simple table
in that book, relating to amputations of the limbs or
parts thereof, appears on the next page.   There are
further sets of tables which allow combinations of
impairments of different parts of the body to be
expressed as impairments of the "whole man".   Thus if a
person lost both an arm and a leg, the medical practitioner would not simply add the percentage for each,
but would combine them in accordance with the tables
provided.   To illustrate: if the amputation of the arm
is such that it constitutes a 60 per cent impairment on
the above table and the amputation of the leg similarly
constitutes a 40 per cent impairment, the combined
values table gives a figure of 76 per cent impairment
of the whole man, which would be certified as 75 per
cent (the nearest multiple of 5).   Since he need merely
"have regard to" the tables, the medical practitioner
is not bound by them and may take into account his own
knowledge of the effect of the incapacity on his
patient.   In any event, many of the tables do leave a
certain amount of discretion to the doctor in arriving
at the degree of impairment within a specified range,
eg in cases of mental illness one finds ranges of 20-45
per cent and 50-85 per cent or more.   The Act requires

TABLE 4—SCHEDULE OF AMPUTATIONS

	Impairment of Whole Man, %
Upper Extremity, Type	
Forequarter amputation	.70
Disarticulation at shoulder joint	.60
Amputation of arm above deltoid insertion	.60
Amputation of arm between deltoid insertion and elbow joint	.57
Disarticulation at elbow joint	.57
Amputation of forearm below elbow joint proximal to insertion of biceps tendon	.57
Amputation of forearm below elbow joint distal to insertion of biceps tendon	.54
Disarticulation at wrist joint	.54
Midcarpal or midmetacarpal amputation of hand	.54
Amputation of all fingers except thumb at metacarpophalangeal joints	.32
Amputation of thumb	
At metacarpophalangeal joint or with resection of carpometacarpal bone	.22
At interphalangeal joint	.16
Amputation of index finger	
At metacarpophalangeal joint or with resection of metacarpal bone	.14
At proximal interphalangeal joint	.11
At distal interphalangeal joint	.6
Amputation of middle finger	
At metacarpophalangeal joint or with resection of metacarpal bone	.11
At proximal interphalangeal joint	.8
At distal interphalangeal joint	.5
Amputation of ring finger	
At metacarpophalangeal joint or with resection of metacarpal bone	.5
At proximal interphalangeal joint	.4
At distal interphalangeal joint	.3
Amputation of little finger	
At metacarpophalangeal joint or with resection of metacarpal bone	3
At proximal interphalangeal joint	2
At distal interphalangeal joint	1
Lower Extremity, Type	
Hemipelvectomy	50
Disarticulation at hip joint	40
Amputation above knee joint with short thigh stump (3 in. or less below tuberosity of ischium)	40
Amputation above knee joint with functional stump	36
Disarticulation at knee joint	36
Gritti-Stokes amputation	36
Amputation below knee joint with short stump (3 in. or less below intercondylar notch)	36
Amputation below knee joint with functional stump	28
Amputation at ankle (Syme's)	28
Partial amputation of foot (Chopart's)	21
Midmetatarsal amputation	14
Amputation of all toes	
At metatarsophalangeal joint	8
Amputation of great toe	
With resection of metatarsal bone	8
At metatarsophalangeal joint	5
At interphalangeal joint	4
Amputation of lesser toe (2nd to 5th)	
With resection of metatarsal bone	2
At metatarsophalangeal joint	1
At proximal interphalangeal joint	0
At distal interphalangeal joint	0

the percentage of incapacity to be expressed as a
multiple of 5, so the doctor would in some instances
have a further discretion to shift the figure upwards
or downwards.

4.305 A person could possibly "shop around" among
medical practitioners and present only the most favourable certificate with his claim for benefits for
permanent partial incapacity. However, the Secretary
may require a beneficiary to undergo an examination by
a specified medical practitioner (s 117(b)), may
require him to furnish information (s 101) - presumably
including the names of doctors who have examined him -
and may require the production of any other medical
certificates (s 102(1)(c)). If he does obtain more
than one certificate, the Secretary may act on whichever of them he considers to be most appropriate
(s 36(1)). An appeal lies against the percentage so
specified (s 38).

4.306 If the person is certified to be 85 per cent
or more incapacitated, benefits are payable as for
total incapacity (see Chap 4, Sec 2). The Report
recommended that generally no benefits should be
payable if the incapacity were certified at 10 per cent
or less (Vol 1, par 401(b)). Again as a result of
pressure from the trade unions - who were concerned
that their members should not be "deprived" of some of
the lump sums now payable under workers' compensation
legislation for the loss of fingers and toes - an
amendment was introduced to the Bill, so that now
section 35(2) provides for the payment of lump-sum
benefits for certain minor injuries. The injuries to
be so compensated and the amount of compensation are to
be prescribed by regulation. At the time of writing no
indication had been given of the likely extent of
compensation for such injuries. The Secretary is also

given a discretion to pay a weekly benefit in the case
of minor incapacities (s 37(2)). Presumably, he would
exercise this discretion in the case of persons whose
earnings were particularly affected by the injury. So
a professional violinist who lost a finger of his left
hand might qualify for a weekly benefit under this
provision.

4.307 Where the percentage of permanent incapacity
is assessed at any multiple of 5 from 15 to 80, a
weekly benefit becomes payable. The committee
recommended that this benefit should not be directly
related to the earnings of the individual who is
incapacitated. It considered that to take into account
the effect of the disability on the actual earnings of
the incapacitated person would reintroduce many of the
disadvantages of the common law. "That method ... is
protracted and expensive. It is nevertheless by no
means certain in its operation and it is productive of
argument and contention. Moreover, it is a serious
impediment to rehabilitation because it discourages an
early return to active work pending a decision upon
the claim" (Report, Vol 1, par 391(b)). It considered
and rejected (ibid, pars 392-5) various other methods
of assessing compensation for permanent partial
incapacity, such as fixed tables for different incapacities. Ultimately (ibid, pars 396-7) it came out in
favour of allowing a percentage of the general average
weekly earnings for males. It saw this as likely to be
fair to all concerned, since it is the lower paid
workers who are usually more likely to have their
earnings affected by physical incapacity. It regarded
this departure from the earnings-related basis of the
scheme as a whole as minimal, affecting only 2 per cent
of beneficiaries, most of whom would be better off
than, or as well off as, if their actual earnings were

used as the basis (ibid, par 399). Finally, it
recommended a discretion to deal with the few remaining
"hard cases" in which a person's actual earnings were
in fact adversely affected beyond the extent of the
benefit payable (ibid, par 398).

4.308   The original Bill accepted the committee's
proposals in full.   Criticism directed at these
provisions led to an amendment (now s 37) designed to
define more closely the circumstances in which the
benefit may be increased.   However, the provisions
remain unsatisfactory.   The committee's aim of ensuring
no loss of income to people partially incapacitated,
but at the same time avoiding individual assessment, is
wholly laudable.   A consequence of its method is,
however, that many people who suffer no loss of income
whatsoever will be compensated for their incapacity.
Such compensation can only be regarded as equivalent to
the common law's compensation for pain and suffering
and loss of amenities.   This in itself cannot be a
cause for complaint.   Yet, once introduce the notion
that some people are entitled to compensation for their
non-pecuniary loss, it becomes unfair to deny such
compensation to others.   Thus those whose earnings are
adversely affected by their incapacities are entitled
to ask that not merely should their pecuniary loss be
made good, but that they should be put in as good a
position as others who have not suffered any pecuniary
loss.   A blue-collar worker is justly indignant if he
and a white-collar worker receive the same benefit for
the loss of a leg, but he alone has suffered reduction
in his earnings, even though, when the benefit is added
to his reduced earnings, he is financially not worse
off than he was before he was injured.

4.309 Be that as it may, the present provisions of
the Act are as follows. A distinction is made between
earners and non-earners, ie between those who earned
some money as an employee or self-employed person
during the year preceding the commencement of their
incapacity and those who did not so earn anything
during the whole of that year. Earners will receive a
weekly benefit equivalent to the degree of their
incapacity (assessed in the manner described in pars
4.304-6) as a percentage of 85 per cent of the average
weekly earnings per employed male unit, seasonally
adjusted, as last published by the Australian
Statistician (ss 33(1) and 4(1)). In the case of non-
earners the base figure is 60 per cent of average
weekly earnings, instead of 85 per cent (s 33(2)). Eg,
if a medical practitioner certifies that a person's
incapacity is 50 per cent and the latest figure for
average weekly earnings before the incapacity commenced
was $150 per week, the benefit payable would be 50 per
cent of 85 per cent of $150, ie 50 per cent of $127.50,
or $63.75, if he were an earner; and 50 per cent of 60
per cent of $150, ie 50 per cent of $90, or $45, in the
case of a non-earner. However, the benefit may not
exceed the benefit payable at the long-term rate for
total incapacity (s 33(3)). Thus, if the example given
were to occur soon after July 1976, when the minimum
figure for earnings had not yet been adjusted above $50
(ss 31 and 95), the non-earner's benefit would be only
$42.50 and not $45.

4.310 Section 33(1) provides that the benefit is
payable only while the incapacity continues, but a
beneficiary may apply to have it determined that the
incapacity is permanent (s 104(2)). Once such determination has been made, the benefit would be payable
until the age of 65 or prior death; unless the

incapacity occurred after the age of 61, in which case
it would be payable for four years or until prior death
(s 18(2)). It could not be reduced or cancelled merely
because the beneficiary unexpectedly improved or even
recovered completely (s 104(2)). It will be increased
automatically each quarter to allow for inflation
(s 94). If a medical practitioner certifies that the
percentage of incapacity has increased, the benefit may
be increased proportionately (s 34). Thus in the
example given in the previous paragraph, if the
earner's incapacity increased from 50 to 60 per cent,
the benefit may be increased from $63.75 to $76.50 per
week. Such increase is not given as of right, but is
left to the discretion of the Secretary. However, a
beneficiary may suffer some different incapacity,
either partial or total. If the benefit to which he
now becomes entitled is higher than that which he was
receiving, the first benefit ceases (s 44). Presumably,
in certifying the degree of incapacity resulting from
the second injury or sickness, the medical practitioner
would take account of the impairment from which he was
already suffering. For example, if a man were receiving a benefit for the loss of a leg when he lost an
arm, the medical practitioner's new certificate would
reflect the percentage impairment of a man who had lost
both a leg and an arm, not of one who had lost an arm
only.

4.311 Section 37(1) provides for payment at a higher
rate, not exceeding that for total incapacity (s 37(6)),
at the discretion of the Secretary where he determines
that, "having regard to the extent to which the
person's personal efficiency and ability to lead a
normal life have been impaired by reason of his
incapacity", the benefit payable is "less than it
should be". In particular, where what the person is

now capable of earning, together with the benefit
payable for permanent partial incapacity, is less than
85 per cent of his pre-injury earnings at the long-term
rate, the Secretary may increase the benefit to bring
the earnings plus benefit up to 85 per cent of the
long-term rate (s 37(3) and (4)). If the Secretary
does determine to pay a higher rate, the increased
benefit itself is subject to increase in the normal way
for inflation (s 37(5)). The Act does not expressly
state whether or not the Secretary may determine to pay
the higher rate temporarily. It is submitted that it
would be out of keeping with the rehabilitative aims of
the scheme to allow benefits at a higher rate to be
temporary; once a determination is made to pay at a
higher rate, the benefit should be treated like any
other and not be subject to reduction (s 104(2)),
except for fraud or mistake (s 104(1); see par 4.106).
These discretionary provisions already constitute a
serious breach of the scheme with regard to rehabilitation, since by involving a determination of what the
incapacitated person is now capable of earning there is
an encouragement to exaggerate the disability. There
is also scope for much dispute: many cases at common
law have shown how difficult it is to resolve the issue
of a plaintiff's post-injury capacity.[1]

Sec 4: DISFIGUREMENT

4.401   Section 51(1) provides: "Where a person has
suffered severe facial or bodily disfigurement and
damages have not been recovered in respect of the
personal injury or sickness that caused the

---

1.   See, eg, the cases referred to in H Luntz, The
     Assessment of Damages for Personal Injury and
     Death (1974), pars 1.1020-2.

disfigurement, the Secretary may determine that there
be paid to that person a benefit by way of a lump-sum
payment of such amount, not exceeding $10,000, as the
Secretary determines." Clearly this applies to people
who have been disfigured before the commencement of the
Act, as long as they have not recovered any damages
(including damages reduced for contributory negligence).
However, the benefit will be payable to people injured
before 1st July 1976 only after point B and to people
disfigured by sickness before point C, only after point
D (s 51(2) and (3); for the meaning of these letters
see par 3.205). There is no provision for the increase
of the maximum of $10,000 to allow for inflation; such
increase would have to be achieved by amendment of the
Act.

4.402 Circumstances for Award. The Report offers
little guidance as to how the discretion to award lump
sums for disfigurement is to be exercised. It merely
states (twice): "There is a need to provide for
cosmetic impairments of real significance. They should
be compensated by a lump sum payment ranging up to a
maximum [payment] of $10,000" (Vol 1, pars 10 and
401(d)). Some of the cases which were decided at
common law in the Supreme Court of New South Wales and
which were included in the Compendium for the purposes
of comparison between common law awards and compensation under the scheme do indicate circumstances in
which the exercise of the discretion would be justified,
but do not indicate the amount likely to be awarded.
The first such case is that of a 17 year old girl bank
clerk who suffered a backward displacement of the right
eye, giving the appearance of a half-closed eye, and
scarring below her right eye and on her nose and temple
area; and who was left with the appearance that one
side of her face is older than the other. Here, as in

all such cases, it is merely stated: "The serious
cosmetic impairment in this case would justify an award
within the range of $0-$10,000 in addition to the
[other benefits]." Two other cases refer to "facial
disfigurement" as a result of blinding and in all the
others there was scarring of parts of the body, such as
the shin, shoulder, face or buttocks.

4.403 It seems reasonably clear then that amputation
of a limb will not itself constitute "disfigurement",
but removal of the outer ear probably would do so.
Severe scarring, whether as the result of burns or
lacerations, would probably be the most frequent
occasion of an award.

4.404 Scale. Where compensation has to be paid for
something which is not commensurable in money, it is
inevitable that some sort of tariff or scale will
develop, with the most severe cases at the top and less
severe ones graded downwards. Where a maximum is fixed
by statute, the question arises whether that maximum is
to be regarded as the appropriate amount for only the
most severe injuries, so that all others must necessarily be compensated by lesser sums. If so, the scale
is, as it were, an internal one, only the relative
degrees of severity and the maximum permissible
compensation being relevant. On the other hand, it may
be relevant to look to outside factors in determining
the appropriate award, the maximum merely providing a
limit beyond which the compensation may not go. If
that is so, there may be a "bunching" of severe cases
at the top of the scale, all being compensated by the
maximum award, whatever their relative degrees of
severity. This is particularly so where the maximum
is, by external criteria, a low one. By way of

illustration[1] one may refer to the experience with the
statutory solatium payable on death to spouses or to
the parents of young children in South Australia.
Although in the days soon after the introduction of the
solatium in 1940 it was said that the statutory maxima
should be treated as the limits of artificial scales
and much effort was expended on distinguishing between
amounts to be awarded, such distinctions became mean-
ingless as inflation eroded the value of money and the
maxima were not increased, except once. Thereafter the
practice developed of merely awarding the maximum to
all plaintiffs. The maximum of $10,000 set for
disfigurement is probably high enough at the present
time to allow a complete gradation and the scale may be
regarded as internally self-sufficient. If, however,
that maximum is not increased, one might find that more
and more cases attract the top award as the value of
money falls.

4.405   Relevant Factors.   In cases at common law the
sex of the victim of disfigurement is often stressed:
the psychological effect on women is likely to be
greater than on men. Such psychological effect in the
case of a girl or young woman may be linked with the
objective fact that a scarred woman is more likely to
lose the chance of marriage than a similarly scarred
man.   Other relevant factors mentioned in damages cases
include the age of the victim (a young child is subject
to teasing); the ease with which the disfigurement can
be disguised and whether it is normally hidden by

---

1.   See H Luntz, The Assessment of Damages for
     Personal Injury and Death (1974), pars 9.602-4.
     Another illustration could be taken from the
     criminal injuries compensation schemes: see
     W T Westling, "Some Aspects of the Judicial Deter-
     mination of Compensation Payable to Victims of
     Crime in Australia" (1974) 48 ALJ 428.

clothing; and the pastimes previously enjoyed, eg
scarring to the body of a swimmer may be more embarrass-
ing than similar scarring to someone who rides horses.
Whether or not the cosmetic damage can be repaired by
plastic surgery should also be relevant under the Act
as much as at common law. How much room there will be
for an individual investigation remains to be seen, but
since the aesthetic consequences have to be judged, it
is difficult to see any standardized approach being
adopted. Individual assessment here is less likely to
harm rehabilitation than elsewhere.

Sec 5: EXPENSES

4.501 Generally. A beneficiary entitled to a
benefit for total or partial incapacity may also
receive reimbursement of "reasonable expenses and
losses necessarily and directly resulting from the
injury" (s 50). Attention has already been drawn (pars
4.207 and 4.303) to the unfortunate limitation of this
provision to beneficiaries, with the consequent
exclusion of self-employed partially disabled persons
and partially disabled housewives. Housewives and
other non-earners totally incapacitated for less than
three weeks would also be excluded, since they would
not be entitled to any other benefit. A child who does
not receive a benefit only because he is below the
qualifying age may nevertheless be paid for expenses he
has incurred (s 50(5)). It appears that the expenses
need not necessarily be incurred during the period for
which the other benefit is payable. Thus persons
qualified to receive benefits for total incapacity
would seem able to obtain reimbursement of expenses
incurred during the "waiting period" (see pars
4.205-7). Expenses incurred by a person who has died

may be recovered by his personal representatives if any
death benefit becomes payable (s 50(1)).

4.502   The amount of reimbursement is in the discretion of the Secretary. It becomes payable only where
the expenses have been paid or the loss has occurred,
though the amount of the loss need not be liquidated
(s 50(2)). It is payable as a lump sum. As only
reasonable expenses and losses necessarily and directly
resulting from the injury or death are payable, it is
difficult to see why these should not be payable as of
right; the only valid reason for the Secretary's
discretion would be so as to exclude losses reimbursed
from other sources. This brings us to the matter dealt
with in the next paragraph.

4.503   Medical and Hospital Expenses. The Report
assumed that most medical and hospital expenses would
fall under the National Health Insurance Scheme and
need not be dealt with under the National Compensation
Scheme (Vol 1, par 372(a)). It did, however, speak of
"appropriate action" being "essential if a general
health scheme is not established before the implementation of the compensation scheme" (ibid, par 372(b)).
Section 50, which permits the payment of compensation
for reasonable expenses and losses necessarily and
directly resulting from injury, does not expressly
exclude medical and hospital expenses. In fact, it
obviously contemplates the inclusion of such expenses,
for subsection (4) provides that the reimbursement of
medical or hospital expenses incurred by Australian
visitors overseas shall not exceed the amount of
corresponding expenses payable in Australia. (This
limitation does not apply to Australians stationed or
studying overseas: they may be reimbursed their
medical and hospital expenses at a higher rate,
provided the expenses are "reasonable".) "Medical

expenses" would presumably include the cost of para-
medical services, such as physiotherapy. Since,
however, all benefits payable under section 50 are
payable only in the discretion of the Secretary,
presumably no reimbursement will be made in respect of
medical and hospital expenses for which reimbursement
may be claimed under the National Health Insurance
Scheme, if that does come into operation. Even if the
National Health Insurance Scheme does not come into
operation, the Secretary might, by refusing to
reimburse medical and hospital expenses where a person
is insured, seek to shift the costs to the private
insurance funds and the State subsidy under the present
arrangements. Yet, since those funds do not pay out
when their members are entitled to compensation, there
may be some difficulty about this. If the major part
of the cost of medical or hospital treatment _is_ met
from health insurance sources, it is unlikely that the
Secretary would reimburse the beneficiary with the
difference between the actual cost and the health
insurance benefit.

4.504 _Express Exclusions_. Section 50(1) expressly
excludes from its scope "expenses or losses in respect
of (a) damage to property; (b) loss of   opportunity
to make a profit; (c) loss from inability to perform a
business or professional contract; or (d) a matter in
respect of which compensation is otherwise payable
under this Act". If damage to property were caused
tortiously, an action could still be brought at common
law, notwithstanding the fact that personal injury was
caused at the same time (_Brunsden_ v _Humphrey_ (1884) 14
QBD 141 (CA)). The losses referred to in (b) and (c),
if resulting from personal injury, could only be sued
for if no benefit at all accrued to the person injured
under the Act (s 97).

4.505 <u>Aids and Appliances</u>. In Volume 2, paragraphs
160-2, of the <u>Report</u> the committee recommended the
establishment of a National Artificial Aids and
Appliances Service to supply, repair and replace equipment appropriate to the needs of the physically or
mentally handicapped, such as "beds, hoists, appliances
and fittings needed in the home for daily living; means
of locomotion, including wheelchairs; special equipment
and tools with which to earn a living; special clothing; special footwear, prosthetic and orthotic aids of
all types; hearing aids; mobility aids for the blind;
and special toilet facilities". The Service would also
be responsible for the alteration of homes to provide
ramps, widened doorways, modified bathrooms, kitchens
and laundries and rails in passages. In the
committee's opinion the "principle should be accepted
that all handicapped persons are entitled to be
supplied with such aids, equipment, appliances and home
alterations as are necessary to bring about a significant improvement in their health and to assist in
their education, mobility and independent living".
Once such a Service is established to fulfil this
admirable aim there will be no cost to the handicapped
person. Meanwhile, however, the purchase of artificial
limbs and other appliances and the adaptation of an
incapacitated person's home or motor car will involve
expense. It seems that reasonable expenses of this
nature, where "necessarily and directly resulting from
the injury", may be reimbursed in a lump sum after they
have been incurred (s 50). One assumes that the
prohibition on payment for "damage to property"
(s 50(1)(a)) would not exclude payment for a new
artificial limb or similar device to replace one
damaged when a person was injured. It would be absurd
that a person who lost his natural limb could claim the

cost of an artificial one, but a person who had his artificial limb damaged in an accident causing physical injury could not claim the cost of replacement.

4.506 Personal Attendant. Section 50(3) singles out for special mention the cost of personal attention for an incapacitated person who requires such attention constantly or intermittently. Domiciliary care is often an important aid to rehabilitation, though no doubt there are limits - established by the requirements that the expenses be reasonable and necessary - which would preclude the provision of an individual private nursing home (cf Cunningham v Harrison [1973] QB 942 (CA)). There are two reasons why the cost of personal attention is specifically referred to in the Act. First, whereas reimbursement of other expenses will normally be made to the beneficiary, payment may here be made direct to the person providing the attention. Secondly, the Report (Vol 1, par 372(d)) contemplates payment for personal attention provided by a member of the beneficiary's family for which the beneficiary would not ordinarily be under any obligation to pay. At common law the Australian courts have on the whole denied a plaintiff the right to recover damages in respect of services rendered on a voluntary basis, but English courts (perhaps influenced by recommendations to this effect by various law reform bodies) have recently allowed recovery in such circumstances (Donnelly v Joyce [1974] QB 454 (CA); P Gerber, "Foreseeable Damages and the Good Samaritan" (1974) 48 ALJ 463).

4.507 Transport Expenses. In the context of aids and appliances the Report (Vol 1, par 372(c)) speaks also of travelling allowances, personal transport and hostel assistance. Payment of many of these expenses under section 50 would become unnecessary if the

committee's recommendations in Volume 2, paragraphs
190-9, were implemented. It is there recommended that
travelling expenses to and from approved courses of
treatment should be paid, that the purchase of
specially adapted vehicles be'subsidized and that an
annual transport allowance be payable to appropriate
persons, who should also be given special driver training and parking facilities.

4.508   Other Matters. Common law cases have allowed
increased laundry costs incurred by paraplegics and
quadriplegics. These will now fall under section 50.
Household help would also come within the section,
provided that the services which it replaces are for a
person who does become entitled to some other benefit
under the Act (see par 4.501). It is difficult,
however, to see what "losses", as distinct from
"expenses", are encompassed. Although the amount of
the loss need not be known, or even ascertainable
(s 50(2)), it must surely be a pecuniary loss and not
the sort of loss compensated at common law under the
heads of pain and suffering, loss of amenities and loss
of expectation of life. The possibility remains that
there may be some loss, not expressly excluded (see par
4.504), for which compensation may be claimed under
section 50.

4.509   Return to Australia. One type of expenditure
is covered under a different section. It is expressly
provided: "Where a benefit is payable to a person
outside Australia, the Secretary may arrange for the
return of that person, and of any member of his family,
to Australia at the expense of Australia" (s 107). For
the circumstances in which a benefit is payable to a
person outside Australia, see paragraphs 3.401-2.

Sec 6:   DEATH

4.601   Funeral Expenses.   The funeral expenses of
people who die by accident on or after 1st July 1976
will be payable under the scheme (s 46).   There is no
provision here for retrospectivity.   The funeral
expenses of people who die as a result of sickness will
only be payable if their death occurs after the scheme
is extended to sickness (s 45).   A lump sum in respect
of the expenses is payable to the person who paid the
cost of the funeral or, if the cost has not been paid,
to the person who carried out the funeral.   The amount
payable is "such amount as the Secretary determines to
be reasonable having regard to the charges customarily
made for funerals in the place where the funeral was
carried out".   The Secretary is also to take into
account "any amount paid or payable in respect of the
cost of the funeral under some other law".   Payment to
the undertaker by the Secretary discharges to that
extent the liability of any other person to the undertaker for the cost of the funeral (s 46(2)).

4.602   The Act does not indicate what costs are to be
allowed for funerals.   Guidance may be obtained from
cases which have interpreted the word "funeral" under
existing statutes that permit the recovery of funeral
expenses from tortfeasors.   In Public Trustee v
Bednarczyk [1959] SASR 178, 180, Mayo J said: "The
word 'funeral' is usually taken to comprehend the
disposal of human remains, including accompanying rites
and ceremonies, that is to say, the procedure of, and
appertaining to, burial or cremation, in the course of
which the body is prepared for burial and conveyed by
cortege to the necropolis.   Such initial stages as
acquisition of burial plot, public notice, obtaining a

certificate of death, permission to cremate or bury, will form part of the procedure and the cost will be funeral expenses." There has been some dispute as to whether the cost of a tombstone is included, but the recent tendency has been to allow it.[1] The cost of at least one wreath and a shroud has also been allowed, but not the cost of transporting the body to a distant place.[2]

4.603 <u>Widows' Benefits</u>. On the death of her husband a widow becomes entitled to certain benefits, whether or not she was dependent on him. The general provisions relating to the phasing-in of the scheme with regard to injury and sickness apply to deaths as a result of those respective causes (see par 3.206). Since the benefits are payable not only to the lawful wives of deceased persons, but also in certain circumstances to "<u>de facto</u> wives" (see par 4.607), it is possible for one man to leave more than one "widow". The Act makes special provision for the sharing of the benefits in such instances. This is discussed in paragraphs 4.608-9; in the other paragraphs hereafter it will be assumed that the deceased left only one "widow", lawful or <u>de facto</u>.

4.604 A widow whose husband dies as a result of injury or sickness after the respective commencing dates for those parts of the scheme, automatically becomes entitled to a lump-sum payment of $1,000 (s 57(1)(a) and (4)(a)). There is no provision for increasing this amount as the value of money falls; if it is to be increased it will have to be done by

---

1. See the cases cited in H Luntz, <u>The Assessment of Damages for Personal Injury and Death</u> (1974), par 9.505.
2. <u>Ibid</u>, par 9.504. A recent case allowing recovery for a wreath is <u>Toth</u> v <u>Wolper</u> (1973) 7 SASR 574.

amendment to the Act. In addition, she immediately
becomes entitled to a weekly pension at the rate of
three-fifths of any pension payable to her husband for
total incapacity at the long-term rate (see pars
4.212-5); if he was not in receipt of such a pension,
then her pension is three-fifths of what his pension
would have been at the long-term rate had he been
totally incapacitated before his death (s 57(1)(b) and
(4)(b)). For example, if the husband's earnings for
the purposes of the long-term rate were an average of
$150 per week at the time of his death, the widow's
pension is 60 per cent of 85 per cent of $150, ie
$76.50 per week. The minimum payable to a widow whose
husband dies as a result of injury after 1st July 1976
will be $51 per week, ie 60 per cent of 85 per cent of
$100 (s 57(2)). This minimum will increase in line
with increases in average weekly earnings (s 95). The
rate for a widow whose husband died from injury before
1st July 1976 is $50 per week (s 58), payable from the
date proclaimed for the commencement of the retrospective part of the injury scheme (s 56(2)(a)). The same
rate of $50 per week will also be paid after point D
(see par 3.205) to widows whose husbands died as a
result of sickness before point C (s 56(2)(b)). Where
there are two "widows" (see pars 4.607-8), each will
receive $50 per week (s 60). The commencing rate of
$50 in the case of retrospective benefits (ss 58 and
60) will not increase automatically with inflation.
The pension itself will in all cases increase in
accordance with the general provisions for inflation
(s 94).

4.605   The length of time for which the pension is
payable depends on whether the widow is a "class A
widow" or a "class B widow". Class A widows have some
impediment to their supporting themselves adequately.

They must be (a) pregnant; (b) maintaining a family
home for a child under 20; (c) caring for an aged or
infirm person who is related by blood or adoption to
the widow; (d) unable to engage in suitable gainful
work; or (e) 55 years old or over (s 55(1)). All other
widows are in class B (ibid). If the conditions
qualifying a widow to be in class A cease to apply, she
transfers to class B; conversely, if conditions (a) to
(d) become applicable to a class B widow, she transfers
to class A. For both classes the pension ceases on
remarriage, though a class A widow receives a "wedding
present" of a lump sum equivalent to the previous
year's pension; if she remarries less than a year after
her husband's death, the lump sum payable to the class
A widow is equivalent to the total pension she has
received. In the absence of a further marriage, the
pension for a class A widow continues until the age of
65 (s 56(3)), or presumably her prior death, unless she
meanwhile transfers to class B. The pension payable to
class B widows ceases after one year if they do not
remarry sooner (s 57(4)(b)). There seems to be no
reason why a widow should not transfer backwards and
forwards between the two classes several times.
However, a class B widow does not transfer to class A
when she attains the age of 55; a woman must have
become a widow after attaining that age to be in class
A (s 55(1)(e)); and she will obviously remain in that
class if she does qualify on this ground. But if a
woman becomes a class A widow before the age of 55 by
reason of maintaining a family home for a child or
caring for an aged or infirm relative, she does not
cease to be in class A if, after she is 55, her
children all reach the age of 20 or leave home or if
the relative dies (s 62(2)).

4.606 Although there has been much criticism of the
limitation of class B widows' pensions to one year,
this provision is fully justifiable. Admittedly, the
common law ultimately took the attitude, after some
hesitation, that generally a widow's ability to earn
for herself is irrelevant to her claim for loss of the
support her husband would probably have provided if he
had not been killed (<u>Carrol</u> v <u>Purcell</u> (1961) 107 CLR
73). Yet that attitude has itself been criticized (eg
A Wharam, "Damages - The Widow's Claim" (1971) 121 NLJ
1064). Widows ought to be encouraged in their own
interests to resume a normal life as soon as possible
and there is no good reason why they should be supported
at community expense when well able to do so themselves.
A widow who is maintaining a home for a child or who is
unable to engage in suitable gainful work would fall
into class A and then the pension would not terminate
after one year.

4.607 "<u>De facto</u> wives", as defined in the Act,
qualify for the above benefits in the same way as women
who are lawfully married. Thus <u>de facto</u> wives may be
either class A or class B widows. To qualify the woman
must have lived with the man for at least three years
immediately before his death or from the time when his
injury or sickness occurred until his death, or there
must be a surviving child of the union who was dependent on the man immediately before his death. In every
case the woman must have been living with the man "on
a permanent and <u>bona fide</u> domestic basis immediately
before his death". A <u>de facto</u> widow (or a lawful widow
for that matter) who forms a similar relationship with
another man is not treated as having "remarried".

4.608   A man who is living on a <u>bona fide</u> and
permanent basis with a woman might have a lawful wife
as well. Thus he might leave two "widows" qualified
for the benefits under the Act. (It would probably be
impossible for there to be more than two, since it is a
necessary condition that a woman not married to the
deceased should have lived with him on a permanent and
<u>bona fide</u> basis immediately before his death, even in
the case where she has a child of the union who was
dependent on the deceased. Nevertheless, the Act makes
provision for "two or more widows" (eg, s 59(6)(b)).)
Each widow receives a lump sum of $1,000 (s 59(2));
they do not share a single lump sum. Where at any time
two widows are qualified to receive a pension, the
Secretary determines the rate payable to each. He does
this "having regard to the extent to which the widow
was dependent on the deceased person immediately before
his death and to any loss suffered by her by reason of
his death" (s 59(3)). However, the total of the two
pensions may not ordinarily exceed the amount payable
if there had been only one (<u>ibid</u>). It may therefore be
expected that the Secretary will normally divide the
full pension proportionately between the widows. The
total payable may in some circumstances be increased,
since it is provided that if the rate of pension
determined to be due to a widow is less than $50, she
is entitled to receive $50 per week (s 59(4)). Thus
the minimum payable when there are two widows will be
$100 per week, though had there been only one widow a
much lower sum would often have been payable. Unlike
other minima, but like the lump sum of $1,000, this $50
is not to be increased for inflation under section 95.
Thus however long after 1st July 1976 a woman's husband
dies, the minimum commencing benefit will be $50 per
week. Once the benefit becomes payable, like all

periodical payments, it will increase each quarter that
it continues to be payable (s 94).

4.609   In some instances the Secretary might determine that the de facto wife was completely dependent on
the deceased, whereas the lawful wife was not at all
dependent.   In such a case, for one year (if either
woman is in class B) or longer (if both are in class A)
or until the marriage of the de facto wife or
remarriage of the lawful one, the total payable would
probably exceed what would otherwise be payable by $50
per week, since the de facto wife should be entitled to
the full pension and the lawful wife to an additional
$50 per week.   It will revert to the amount of the
ordinary pension if one marries or, after a year, if
either woman is in class B or, where they are both in
class A, if one transfers to class B (s 59(6)).   If one
ceases to be eligible for a pension, but subsequently
again becomes a class A widow, the amount of the
pension payable to each has again to be calculated
(s 59(7)).   Even where no extra amount is being paid;
but the two widows share the full pension, on one of
them ceasing to be eligible, the other becomes entitled
to the full amount, whatever the degree of her dependency on the deceased (s 59(6)(a)).   This is in accordance with the provisions where a man dies leaving only
one widow: she is entitled to the full pension even if
she was not dependent on him at all.

4.610   A widow's pension payable as a result of the
death of her husband is not affected if she herself
should be incapacitated and become entitled to a
benefit for total or partial incapacity (s 62(1)).
However, the pension may have to abate proportionately
if the total payable to her and to the children of the
deceased (as described in the succeeding paragraphs)
would otherwise exceed the amount which would have been

paid to the husband on total incapacity (s 61). Since
the widow normally receives 60 per cent of the amount
that would have been so payable (s 57(1)(b)), abatement
will be necessary only where the children would receive
more than 40 per cent, ie when there are three or more
eligible children (s 47(1)(a)). It is submitted that
section 61, providing for proportionate abatement in
such cases, must be read subject to section 57(2),
which prescribes a minimum of $100 (as increased from
time to time under s 95) for the earnings on which the
calculation is to be based (Report, Vol 1, par 384(h)).

4.611 Children's Benefit. Legitimate children of a
deceased man who are under the age of 20 but have not
completed their full-time education (s 25(1)), and, if
girls, are not married (s 49), are entitled to a
benefit on his death, whether they were dependent on
him or not. Legitimate children of a woman or her
husband are entitled to a benefit on her death only if
they (a) are under 20, (b) have not completed their
full-time education, (c) are not married women, and
(d) were substantially dependent on her immediately
before her death (s 47(5)). Illegitimate children have
to satisfy a test of dependency to claim in respect of
the death of their father or their mother or a former
spouse of a parent (s 25(2)). Adopted and foster
children are included with other legitimate ones
(s 47(1)). The benefits will be phased in in the same
way as other benefits (ss 45 and 47(4); see par 3.206).
Where a child's father, or his mother on whom he was
dependent, died before 1st July 1976 as a result of
injury, $13 per week will become payable to the child
after point B (see par 3.205); this is doubled if the
other parent is also dead (s 47(3) and (4)(a)).
Similar sums become payable after point D in respect of
deaths as a result of sickness before point C.

4.612   In the case of death as a result of injury and
sickness after the respective commencing dates for
those parts of the scheme, the rate of benefit for each
child, irrespective of the degree of dependency, is 15
per cent of the long-term rate for total incapacity
(s 47(1)(a)).   It is doubled if both parents are dead
(s 47(1)(b)).   As with the widows' pension, if the
earnings on which the long-term rate are calculated are
less than $100, the calculation is to be based on earn-
ings of $100 (s 47(2)).   This figure of $100 will
increase in line with average weekly earnings (s 95).
Thus an only child would receive a minimum of $12.75
per week, ie 15 per cent of 85 per cent of $100 per
week on the death of his father, and $25.50 per week if
his mother were already dead.   Where there are a number
of children, as well as a widow, the amount payable to
each may have to abate proportionately if the total
otherwise payable would exceed what would have been
paid to the deceased on total incapacity (s 61).   Again
it is submitted that this provision for abatement must
be read subject to the provision that the minimum earnings of the deceased for the basis of the calculation
are to be taken at $100 per week (s 47(2);   see par
4.610).

4.613   Illustrations.   Assume a family where the
father, who earned an average of $150 per week in the
year before his death, was killed after 1st July 1976.
The widow's pension, as we have seen (par 4.604), is
$76.50 per week (in addition to the lump sum of $1,000).
If there are one or two children, each receives a
benefit of $19.13 per week.   If there are three
children, since the total may not exceed $127.50 (85
per cent of $150), the widow's pension and the benefit
payable to each child abate proportionately.   Thus the
widow receives $72.86 and each child $18.21 per week.

If there are four children, the widow receives $63.75
and each child $15.94 per week. If their mother is
already dead, one, two or three children each receives
$38.25 per week; four or more children would share
$127.50 per week equally among them. The benefits
payable will increase each quarter to allow for
inflation (s 94). Presumably, in cases where there has
been an abatement, as each child reaches the age of 20
or completes his full-time education or, if a girl,
marries - and so becomes ineligible for the benefit -
the amount payable to the widow and each other child
increases until it reaches 60 per cent and 15 per cent
respectively of what would have been paid to the
deceased on total incapacity.

4.614 <u>Widowers</u>. Except as described in the next
paragraph, no benefit is payable to a widower on the
death of his wife (see the definition of the classes of
widow in s 55(1)). Nor would any benefit be payable to
her children unless they were substantially dependent
on her (s 47(5)). This is an unfortunate omission. At
common law an action lies against a wrongdoer for the
loss of the services of a wife and mother. If this
action survives (see par 3.104) the husband and
children of a woman killed by the negligence of another
person will be favoured over other equally innocent
bereaved families, at least if the tortfeasor is
insured or is able to pay the damages himself. If the
action does not survive there will be a gap in meeting
the needs of all such families. The scheme should
provide for the reasonable cost of employing a house-
keeper in appropriate circumstances.

4.615 <u>Relatives' Benefit</u>. Widowers, including men
who were living with women as their <u>de facto</u> husbands
(s 48(5)), are included among the relatives who may
claim compensation in the circumstances set out in

section 48. Others included are relatives of the
deceased person by blood or adoption, not being
children eligible for the children's benefit or de
facto wives eligible for the widow's pension (s 4(1)).
Adult children may thus qualify. So may relatives
presently excluded from actions under Lord Campbell's
Act, eg a nephew who was being put through university
by his uncle who has been killed. Relatives over the
age of 65 are excluded (ibid). The benefit is payable
only where the Secretary is satisfied that the relative
was dependent on the deceased person at the time of his
or her death (s 48(1)).

4.616 The amount of the benefit payable to a dependent relative is entirely within the discretion of the
Secretary. He may award a lump sum of any amount or a
weekly payment at any rate he determines from time to
time (s 48(2)). He is required to have regard to (a)
the extent to which the relative has suffered economic-
ally by the death of the deceased person; (b) the state
of his health; (c) his age; (d) his ability to engage
in suitable gainful work; (e) the nature and extent of
his income; (f) the total of the rates of benefit (if
any) payable to the widow (or widower) and children of
the deceased person; and (g) such other matters as he
considers to be appropriate (s 48(3)). Presumably an
adult child of a wealthy father who, because of his own
congenital total incapacity, was receiving the minimum
benefit under section 41 and was also being supported
by his father, would be entitled to a benefit under
section 48 on the death of his father. In determining
the benefit in such a case the Secretary could no doubt
take into account any benefits the child might receive
from his father's estate.

4.617 Any weekly benefit awarded to a relative by
the Secretary continues until the Secretary determines
that it is no longer necessary (s 48(4)(a)). In the
absence of such a determination it will continue until
the beneficiary reaches the age of 65, or, if he was
already 64 when the relative on whom he was dependent
died, for one year (s 48(4)(b)). Benefits payable
under this section are not to be increased on account
of inflation (s 48(6)).

Sec 7: OTHER MATTERS

4.701 _Inflation_. Perhaps more than with any other
difficulty, the common law method of awarding damages
has failed to cope with the problem of the accelerated
rate of inflation in recent years. The solution
adopted by the Woodhouse committee is to provide for
automatic adjustments each quarter in the level of the
major periodical benefits being distributed under the
National Compensation Scheme. It also provides for the
automatic increase each year of the important minimum
and maximum figures used in the calculation of benefits.
The method of adjusting the level of benefits already
being paid is by reference to increases in the consumer
price index, together with a notional allowance for
increased prosperity in the rest of the community due
to greater productivity. The maximum and minimum
figures, on which the commencing rate of benefits
payable in particular cases is based, are increased by
reference to increases in average weekly earnings per
employed male unit, which criterion would normally
contain built-in factors allowing both for higher cost
of living and real improvements in living standards.
Unfortunately, these latter adjustments will start
operating only one year after the scheme comes into

force. Even if the figures suggested by the Woodhouse
committee in July 1974 were adequate - and there is
reason to doubt the adequacy of the basic figure of $50
on which the benefits payable to non-earners is
calculated - it is unlikely that they will be anywhere
near adequate in the year from 1st July 1976 to 30th
June 1977. Since the figures used during that first
year constitute the base on which subsequent increases
are built, the minimum level of benefits may always be
too low. It is therefore suggested that before the
scheme comes into operation, the maximum and minimum
figures in the Act should be amended to take account of
inflation between 1974 and 1976.

4.702 <u>Important Distinctions</u>. It is important to
distinguish between the calculation of the initial rate
of benefit to which a person becomes entitled (whether
for total incapacity or on the death of a husband or
father) and the subsequent rates. In the calculation
of the initial rate of benefit, regard may have to be
had to different minima (depending, for instance, on
whether it is an incapacity or death benefit) and a
maximum. Such minima and maximum will vary in line
with average weekly earnings, as set out in paragraph
4.704. It should be noted that the calculation of the
initial rate of benefit for permanent partial
incapacity, within the minimum and maximum range, may
also be dependent on average weekly earnings: in this
instance the average weekly earnings last published
before the benefit begins to be payable (s 33(1)).
Once the initial rate of benefit has been calculated,
increases in average weekly earnings become irrelevant
to that beneficiary: his rate varies in line with the
consumer price index, as set out in paragraph 4.703.

4.703   <u>Weekly Benefits</u>.   The rate of benefit payable
to each beneficiary who is in receipt of weekly payments (except the discretionary relatives' benefit:
s 48(6); par 4.617) is automatically increased each
quarter by the percentage increase in the consumer
price index plus one-quarter of one per cent (s 94).
For instance, assume that a beneficiary shortly after
1st July 1976 becomes entitled to a weekly benefit of
$100 per week and that in the quarter ending on 30th
September 1976 the consumer price index has increased
by 4 per cent (ie at an annual rate of 16 per cent).
From the 1st November the weekly benefit payable will
be $104.25.   On the first day of the second month of
each subsequent quarter the benefit will again be
increased as a result of a similar calculation.   Should
it ever happen that there is no increase in the
consumer price index during a particular quarter, the
benefit will still be increased by 0.25 per cent.   Even
if the consumer price index were to fall, there would
be no reduction in the weekly benefit, but an increase
of 0.25 per cent (s 94(2)).   Following a temporary
decrease in the consumer price index, the percentage
increase is calculated by reference to the last quarter
in relation to which the benefits were increased
(s 94(5)).   For example, say the consumer price index
moved as follows during the quarters of one year: 200,
204, 202, 206.   After the second quarter benefits would
be increased by 2.25 per cent; after the third quarter
by 0.25 per cent; and after the fourth quarter by 1.24
per cent.   For the purposes of these calculations the
consumer price index to be used is "the all groups
consumer price index number for the weighted average of
the six State capital cities published by the [Common-
wealth] Statistician" (s 93(1)).   Provision is made for

changes in the published figures and the reference base
used (s 93(2) and (3)).

4.704 <u>Maximum and Minimum Figures</u>. In calculating
the initial rate of benefit during the first year of
operation of the scheme the following maximum and
minimum figures may be relevant: maximum earnings of
$500 and the minimum notional earnings of $50 per week
for the purpose of calculating benefits on total
incapacity (s 31; par 4.210); minimum notional earnings
of $50 per week for the benefit payable after the first
four weeks during the phases of the scheme before the
introduction of retrospective benefits (s 41(2); par
4.212); and minimum earnings of $100 per week for the
purpose of calculating the widow's pension and
children's benefit (ss 57(2) and 47(2); pars 4.604 and
4.612). After the scheme has been operating for a year,
and in each subsequent year, each of these figures is
to be increased by the percentage increase from one
March quarter to the next in average weekly earnings
per employed male unit in Australia, seasonally
adjusted, as published by the Commonwealth Statistician
(ss 95 and 4(1)). For example, if the average weekly
earnings for the March quarter in 1976 is $150 and by
the March quarter in 1977 it has risen to $180, ie by
20 per cent, then the maximum and minimum earnings for
the purpose of calculating the benefit for total
incapacity will be $600 and $60 respectively from 1st
July 1977. In the unlikely event that there is no
increase in average weekly earnings, or the increase is
less than 1 per cent, the figures will still be
increased by 1 per cent.

4.705 The rate of benefit for total incapacity is,
of course, usually 85 per cent of the person's own
average earnings at either the short-term or long-term
rate (pars 4.210 and 4.213), subject to a maximum of 85

per cent of $500 as increased from year to year in the
manner described in the previous paragraph.   The
minimum of 85 per cent of $50, as so increased, does
not apply to actual earners; it is a notional figure to
be applied to people not in full-time employment.   For
full-time employees a separate minimum will be prescribed; low wage earners may then receive a benefit of
100 per cent of their average earnings up to the amount
so prescribed (s 42; par 4.214).

4.706   Additional Cover.   Any person who is concerned
that 85 per cent of his own average earnings or 85 per
cent of $500 per week (as increased in the manner
described in par 4.704) will not sufficiently compensate him should he be totally incapacitated is free to
contract with an insurance company or his employer for
additional benefits.   Personal accident insurance and
industrial bargaining for make-up payments are not
prohibited under the Act.   Life assurance may still be
thought to be necessary to provide long-term advantages
for one's dependants, though they are able to support
themselves.   If the Act is not amended, insurance
against temporary partial disability will be essential
for many self-employed people.   A concert-pianist will
still no doubt want to insure himself against permanent
injury to his hands; there is nothing to prevent him
doing so.

Chapter 5

ADMINISTRATION

Sec 1: LODGEMENT AND ASSESSMENT OF CLAIMS

5.101 Administration by Government Department. The Report (Vol 1, par 405(a)) recommended the establishment of a central social welfare policy group within the Australian Government, designed to co-ordinate activities across the full range of the social welfare area. Under the central policy group would fall divisions dealing with (a) the provision of compensation benefits and allowances (including assessments); (b) all aspects of rehabilitation, whether medical, vocational, social or educational; (c) health and welfare services (excluding rehabilitation services); (d) safety; and (e) health standards. The provision of compensation under the proposed scheme would be coupled with the provision of various other social security benefits. The committee rejected the idea that the scheme could be administered effectively either by private insurers or an independent commission (see generally Chap XXVII of Vol 1 of the Report). It expressed confidence that "men with the right administrative experience and breadth of intellect to control the operation in its early days ... can and will be found" (ibid, par 407(c)).

5.102   "<u>The Secretary</u>".   The Act places the function
of assessing and providing compensation within the
Department of Repatriation and Compensation.   As will
have been apparent from Chapter 4, many of the tasks
relating to assessment are required to be performed by
"the Secretary".   He is defined as the Permanent Head
of the Department of Repatriation and Compensation
(s 4(1)).   Obviously he will not perform these multi-
tudinous tasks personally.   The Act provides that he
may establish offices at such places as he thinks fit
and place an officer in charge of any such office (s 6).
Subject to the directions of the Secretary and to his
power of review, any officer (ie a person employed in
the Department (s 4(1)), not necessarily the officer in
charge) may exercise any of the powers of the Secretary
under the Act (s 7).

5.103   <u>Lodgement of Claims</u>.   Section 63 provides that
a benefit is not payable unless a claim in writing is
lodged, in the manner prescribed by regulation, by or
on behalf of the beneficiary.   No doubt, the regulations
will be simple, in keeping with the committee's
recommendation "that any request for a benefit, no
matter how informal, should be treated as an application, provided the few essential particulars of name,
nature of incapacity, place of residence and some
particulars of medical treatment were included,
together with a signature by or on behalf of the
applicant" (<u>Report</u>, Vol 1, par 416(a)).   It would then
be up to the Department "to communicate with the
medical authority concerned or to embark upon any other
appropriate inquiry" (<u>ibid</u>).   An alternative method of
applying for benefits will be simply by lodging, again
in the manner prescribed by regulation, a certificate
by a medical practitioner specifying the name of the

incapacitated person and particulars of his personal injury or sickness (s 64). No time limit is laid down for lodging a claim by either method (Report, Vol 1, par 416(c)).

5.104 It may be contemplated, however, that, if not on the initial application, at some stage information relating to the circumstances in which injuries occurred will be sought. Until now Australian statistics on injuries "have been inadequate and often misleading" (Report, Vol 2, par 309). In consequence, research aimed at accident prevention has been much hampered. "The introduction of a comprehensive compensation scheme for all significant injuries provides a unique and important opportunity for developing meaningful statistics concerning all accidents" (ibid, par 310).

5.105 Investigation of Claims. The Report (Vol 1, par 417(a)) states: "In fairness to applicants, to avoid contention, and for reasons of good administration it is essential that the methods used to process and consider applications should be both flexible and speedy. In addition, those concerned should adopt a helpful and sensibly tolerant attitude in discharging their responsibilities." Flexibility is ensured by the Act providing that a "claim shall be investigated as the Secretary thinks appropriate" (s 65). That is reinforced, and speed is encouraged, by section 69(1), which requires the Secretary to "act with as little formality and technicality and with as much expedition as the requirements of this Act and a proper consideration of the real merits and justness of the claim or matter permit". If the Secretary does not inform the applicant within 21 days after the claim has been lodged of the decision that it is proposed to make, a request may be made that the matter be dealt with by an

Appeal Tribunal (as to which, see Sec 2 of this Chapter) (s 69(2)). The Secretary must then, within seven days, either inform the applicant of the proposed decision or refer the matter to an appropriate Appeal Tribunal (s 69(3)). (The reason why these subsections refer to "the decision that it is proposed to make" rather than simply "the decision" will appear from pars 5.109-10.)

5.106 Whether or not the practice of the officials administering the scheme lives up to these ideals of flexibility and speed, sympathy and tolerance, remains to be seen. There has been much criticism of the scheme on the ground that it will introduce intolerant bureaucracy. With good will and effort on the part of the officers of the Department of Repatriation and Compensation this criticism will prove unfounded. According to a report in The Age of 7th January 1975 the Department might use the compensation of injured victims of the Darwin cyclone disaster as a trial run for the scheme. It is to be hoped that any such trial proves successful. By way of comparison, one should remember that under the present common law system, probably over 85 per cent of claims are settled. Most of these are settled by clerks and officials of insurance companies, who can be every bit as bureaucratic as Government employees. Litigated claims involve dreadful delays. From the Compendium, Part IV, Table 9, it may be seen that approximately 90 per cent of such claims are not paid within one year, between 25 and 44 per cent are not paid within three years, and in New South Wales 14.9 per cent are still unpaid after five years. Any benefits these claimants might have been receiving under workers' compensation or no-fault motor accident schemes will long have been exhausted before the common law damages, if recovered at all, will be paid.

5.107 <u>Interim Payments</u>. Pending a decision on a
claim, the Secretary may authorize an interim payment
at such rate as he determines (s 70(1). If it subsequently turns out that the applicant was not entitled
to the benefit, or was entitled to a benefit at a lower
rate, there is no obligation to refund the amount
received or the excess (s 70(2)). If in fact the
applicant was entitled all along to a higher rate of
benefit, the extra money must later be paid to him
(s 70(3)). Again these provisions are to be contrasted
with the common law where, by withholding all payments,
insurance companies can often force a desperate
claimant into an unfavourable settlement.

5.108 <u>Taking Evidence</u>. In order to investigate a
claim the officials of the Department may need evidence
of the applicant's earnings, medical condition and
other matters. For this purpose, and for other
purposes of the Act, the Secretary is empowered to (a)
summon witnesses; (b) receive evidence on oath or
affirmation; and (c) require the production of documents
(s 102(1)), subject to the sanction of a fine of $200
(s 102(2)). Statements or disclosures made by witnesses
in such circumstances are not admissible in civil or
criminal proceedings against them (s 102(3)), though,
if they fraudulently make false or misleading statements, they may be prosecuted and punished with a fine
of up to $1,000 or imprisonment for up to six months
(s 108). The Secretary is also given power to require
a person whom he believes to be in a position to do so,
to furnish a confidential report on a matter that might
affect the grant or payment of a benefit (s 111). The
person to whom such a request is directed by post must
reply within 14 days and the report must not be false
or misleading (<u>ibid</u>). The penalty for failure to
furnish a report, or for furnishing one that is false

or misleading, is $200 (ibid). This power to require a
report is not expressly subject to the safeguard that
it may not be used in evidence against the witness, but
the fact that it is "confidential" may have the same
effect. Nor is it expressly stated that the penalty
for a false or misleading report may be imposed only if
it is made "with fraudulent intent", as is required
under section 108. It may be that such a requirement
would be implied, though whether the onus of proving
such intent would rest on the Crown, or the accused
would have to show that he acted innocently, is a
controversial question.[1] The right of the Secretary to
obtain information or a report overrides any other law
creating confidentiality (s 112). Subject to certain
circumstances in which they may be authorized to
divulge information (s 103(4)), officers are required
to observe secrecy with regard to information they
acquire in the performance of their duties (s 103). An
applicant or a beneficiary, however, is always entitled
to all information by reference to which the Secretary
acted (s 106).

5.109 Adverse Decisions. The Report (Vol 1, par 417)
stressed the need to give applicants every reasonable
opportunity to provide all favourable information.
"Precipitate decisions against applicants are
unnecessary and could lead to numerous appeals that
otherwise would have been avoided" (ibid, par 417(b)).
The committee therefore recommended that only favourable decisions on applications should be communicated
to applicants and that, if the initial reaction was
adverse, "the file should go automatically for review

---

1. See P Brett, "Strict Responsibility: Possible
    Solutions" (1974) 37 Mod L Rev 417 and the author-
    ities and contrary views there referred to.

by a senior departmental officer or officers" (ibid, par 417(d)). Even if the senior officers were of the same opinion, the decision against the applicant would still not be made immediately, but he would "be told in writing that while no decision had yet been taken, it seemed unlikely on the information presently available (and for short reasons given in the letter) that the application could be granted" (ibid, par 417(e)). The letter would also inform him of his right to be heard in person, with or without representation, or to present further information in writing, whereupon the matter would be considered afresh.

5.110 The Act, while authorizing the procedures set out in the previous paragraph, does not spell out the matter in quite so much detail. It requires the Secretary to inform the applicant in writing of all proposed decisions (apparently favourable ones as well as adverse) and of his right to be heard and to present further evidence (s 66(1)). There is nothing expressly to require a senior officer to review the proposed adverse determination of a junior clerk before the sending of this letter. However, the "Secretary may, of his own motion, reconsider a claim and, if it is proposed to make a decision different from the proposed decision of which the applicant has already been informed, he shall again inform the applicant" (s 66(2)). This may speed up the procedure, since the review by the senior officers could take place at the same time as the first letter is going out to the applicant and the latter is considering whether to request a hearing.

5.111 An applicant informed of a proposed decision has a month within which to request reconsideration (s 67(1)). The Secretary may extend this period of one month (ibid). The request is to be in the manner

prescribed by regulation. If no such request is made,
the proposed decision is confirmed in writing (ss 66(3)
and 68(1)). If a request is made it may set out
reasons in support of the request (s 67(2)), but such
reasons are not obligatory.

5.112 <u>Reconsideration</u>. The Act merely provides
(s 67(3)): "The Secretary shall, if the applicant so
requests, give to the applicant an opportunity of being
heard in person or by a person acting on his behalf and
of furnishing further information to the Secretary."
The <u>Report</u> (Vol 1, par 418(a)) indicates that a
"departmental inquiry should be conducted by two
officers specifically designated to undertake the task.
One should have a legal background of suitable quali-
fication". Since the assessment should be made
speedily, "there will be a need for the departmental
tribunals to be accessible and sufficiently numerous to
be able to deal with requests for a hearing without
delay" (<u>ibid</u>, par 418(d)). There would apply to the
inquiry the requirement of the Act that the Secretary
shall act with as little formality and technicality as
a proper consideration of the real merits and justness
of the claim permit (s 69(1); par 5.105). The <u>Report</u>
(Vol 1, par 418(b)) spells this out:

> The inquiry should be quite informal; the process
> should be that of inquiry; the facts should be
> surveyed from both points of view on the basis of
> discussion rather than argument; and the depart-
> mental officers should endeavour to ensure that
> every reasonable assistance had been given an
> applicant in order to understand and deal with all
> relevant considerations. In particular, a copy of
> any medical report in the hands of the Department
> should be made available to the applicant
> concerned.

5.113 <u>Decision</u>. Once the matter has been reconsidered a decision is made (s 67(4)). The applicant
must be informed of the decision in writing (s 68(1)).
Unless the decision is wholly in his favour, the
applicant must be given reasons and be informed that he
may appeal against it. The <u>Report</u> (Vol 1, par 418(c))
states that the powers of the Appellate Tribunal should
be explained to him, including those with regard to
costs.

Sec 2: APPEALS

5.201 <u>Right of Appeal</u>. A general right of appeal
against all decisions of departmental officers is given
to "applicants", ie persons who have lodged a claim or
on behalf of whom a claim has been lodged (s 4(1)). In
particular, section 82 makes provision for an appeal
against the decisions discussed in the previous Section.
All other decisions and determinations of the Secretary
or his officials may be appealed against under section
105 (see the definition of "determination" in s 4(1)).
An appeal also lies against a certificate of a medical
practitioner on which the Secretary acted for the
purposes of determining the degree of a person's
permanent incapacity (s 38). A proposed decision under
section 115 to suspend payment of a benefit to a
beneficiary who is imprisoned or hospitalized or to pay
the benefit to some other person (par 4.106) is also
subject to appeal (s 115(5)). The manner of lodging an
appeal, and the time within which it is to be lodged,
are to be prescribed by regulations (s 82(1)); that
time may be extended (s 82(2)).

5.202 Appeal Tribunal. The appeal in all these
cases is to a specially constituted Appeal Tribunal.
The Report (Vol 1, par 421(b)) recommended that the
Appeal Tribunals should be completely independent,
their personnel and staff not being part of the
compensation department, but under the jurisdiction of
the Attorney-General's Department. However, the Act
provides for the establishment of as many Appeal
Tribunals as "the Minister" considers necessary and, in
terms of the Acts Interpretation Act 1901-73, s 17(i),
this means the Minister for the time being administering the Act, ie the Minister for Repatriation and
Compensation. In other respects the Tribunals will
almost certainly be independent of the Department. The
actual members are to be appointed by the Governor-
General and the chairman of each Tribunal is to be a
barrister or solicitor of at least five years' standing
(s 71). Although the Report (Vol 1, par 421(a))
recommended that one should be a medical practitioner,
the Act does not specify the qualifications of the
other two members of each Tribunal. The members are to
be full-time (s 72), must be appointed for a specified
period of up to five years and may be re-appointed
thereafter (s 73(1)). The salary of members is to be
determined by the Remuneration Tribunal (s 75(1)).
There are very limited powers of suspension or removal
from office on the grounds of misbehaviour, physical or
mental disability or bankruptcy (s 78). The Report
(Vol 1, par 421(f)) contemplates the setting up of
Appeal Tribunals in each of the capital cities and the
holding of hearings in other places. This is possible
under sections 71 and 81.

5.202A <u>Procedure</u>. Like the departmental officers
(s 69(1); par 5.105), the members of the Appeal
Tribunal are required to conduct their proceedings
"with as little formality and technicality and with as
much expedition as the requirements of this Act and a
proper consideration of the real merits and justness of
the matters and questions before the Tribunal permit"
(s 83(1)). The Tribunal is not bound by any rules of
evidence (s 83(2)). This is an entirely proper
provision, commonly found in statutes setting up administrative tribunals. Most of the rules of evidence
were created in the days when all trials were before
juries and most jurymen were illiterate. A prominent
English Queen's Counsel, perhaps somewhat tongue-in-
cheek, but with a basis of truth, has said that "there
never was a more slapdash, disjointed and inconsequent
body of rules than that which we call the Law of
Evidence. Founded apparently on the propositions that
all jurymen are deaf to reason, that all witnesses are
presumptively liars and that all documents are presumptively forgeries, it has been added to, subtracted
from and tinkered with for two centuries until it has
become less of a structure than a pile of builders'
debris" (C P Harvey, <u>The Advocate's Devil</u> (1958), 79).
Although the Tribunal is authorized to take evidence on
oath (s 86(1)(a)), the <u>Report</u> (Vol 1, par 421(d))
suggests that, except in rare circumstances, witnesses
should not be obliged to give evidence on oath.
"Informal and simple procedures should be the key to
all appeals. The approach should be of an inquisitorial
nature and adversary techniques should not be used"
(<u>ibid</u>).

5.203   The proceedings will generally be in public
(s 84(1)), but confidential matters can be dealt with
in private (ss 84(2) and 38(2)); and where the Tribunal
exercises the function of the Secretary after the
latter has failed within the specified time to deal
with an initial application (par 5.105) the proceedings
must be in private (s 69(6)).   As before the departmental inquiry (par 5.112), the applicant has the right
to be heard and is entitled to be represented by a
member of the legal profession or any other person
(s 82(4); Report, Vol 1, par 421(e)).   The Tribunal may
award the applicant his costs and expenses or part
thereof (s 90).   He cannot be required to pay costs.

5.204   Decision of Tribunal.   The Appeal Tribunal is
required to give reasons for its decision, including
its findings on material questions of fact (s 82(5)).
A notice of its decision and reasons must be given to
the Secretary and to the applicant (ibid).   Since it
may exercise all the powers that the Secretary has
under the Act (s 85), the Tribunal may substitute its
own decision for any decision or determination made by
departmental officers or the Secretary himself.   The
officers are then required to give effect to the
decision (s 82(6)).   Similarly, the Secretary is
required to give effect to the Tribunal's decision on
an appeal against the degree of incapacity certified in
the certificate of a medical practitioner on which the
Secretary acted (s 38(3)).

5.205   Further Appeal.   On issues of fact no further
appeal is permitted.   However, an appeal lies to a
court against any "decision of an Appeal Tribunal that
involves a question of law" (s 92(1)).   Either the
Secretary or the applicant may appeal.   The court to
which such an appeal may be taken is the Superior Court
of Australia, which will presumably be established by

the time the Act comes into operation. If it has not
been established by then, an amendment to the Act will
be needed. The requirement that the Tribunal give
reasons for its decision opens the way for many such
appeals. The restriction of appeals to questions of
law under workers' compensation legislation[1] seems only
occasionally to prevent appeals to the courts;[2] one
frequently finds before the Supreme Court cases stated
in a form - such as "whether, on the facts as found,
there was evidence to support" a particular conclusion
- which differ only marginally from appeals on questions
of fact.[3]

5.206 Appeal to Court. Where an appeal to the
Superior Court lies, because it involves a question of
law or the issue is sufficiently dressed up to look
like one, adversary proceedings are introduced for the
first time. The parties to the appeal are the applicant
and the Secretary (s 92(2)). It is to be heard and
determined by a single judge (s 92(3)), who may admit
further evidence (s 92(4)). The court has a discretion
to order either party to pay costs to the other party
(s 92(6)). "The decision of the court is final and
conclusive" (s 92(7)). If the Superior Court of
Australia Bill 1973 becomes law in its present form, a
further appeal will lie from the single judge to the
Full Court, since clause 21(1) provides for such an

---

1.   Eg, Workers Compensation Act 1958 (Vic), s 56;
     Workers' Compensation Act 1926 (NSW), s 37.
2.   Eg, Buckle v Commonwealth Aircraft Corporation Pty
     Ltd [1968] VR 359 (FC). Of course, many potential
     appeals on questions of fact may be inhibited by
     legal advice that they cannot be brought.
3.   Eg, Stokes v OK Soft Drinks Pty Ltd [1973] VR 454
     (FC); Bill Williams Pty Ltd v Williams (1972) 46
     ALJR 285; Darling Island Stevedoring & Lighterage
     Co Ltd v Hankinson (1967) 117 CLR 19.

appeal and clause 21(2) states that this shall apply
"notwithstanding any other law". Furthermore, clause
38(1) provides for an appeal, by leave, from the Full
Court to the High Court of Australia "[n]otwithstanding
any other Act". One might echo here the words of
Dean J in relation to a Victorian statute providing
that an appeal shall be "final and conclusive"
(Achilleos v Housing Commission [1960] VR 164, 169):

> It is unfortunate that Parliament still continues
> to use an expression which led the Privy Council
> in the Fitzroy Case [[1901] AC 153] to say, at
> p. 163: "It is a hazardous use of language, and
> difficulties have sprung from it in other statutes
> and other departments of law; but it seems to have
> found favour in Victoria". It would seem better
> that Parliament should say quite clearly what it
> means instead of using doubtful expressions.

The procedure before the Superior Court will, of course,
be the ordinary procedure of the court: here there is
no requirement of informality or freedom from technicality.

Chapter 6

MISCELLANEOUS

Sec 1: CONSTITUTIONAL VALIDITY

6.101 The powers of the Federal Parliament are, of course, limited and considerable doubt must exist as to whether all the provisions of the National Compensation Scheme are constitutionally valid. The Report itself is strangely silent on the question. Although the index to Volume 1 contains a heading "Constitution" under which it lists various issues which could be constitutionally controversial, the text to which one is there referred contains little to enlighten one as to how a challenge in the High Court of Australia could be effectively withstood. However, Professor G W R Palmer, principal assistant to the committee, has said[1] that "the committee had available to it a variety of eminent constitutional opinion and it was advised that its proposals were within power".

6.102 It is to be hoped that the attitude to this issue taken by one of the most outspoken critics of the draft Bill, Mr K H Marks QC, will prevail generally. He has on at least two occasions, when discussing the Bill at seminars, declined to answer questions

---

1. In a paper, "Accidents, Sickness and Compensation: The Direction of Social Welfare in Australia", delivered to the annual meeting of the Australian Universities Law Schools Association held at Monash University in August 1974.

concerning its constitutional validity and has instead
expressed the hope that it would be judged on its
merits: if it were thought beneficial to the Australian
people as a whole, it ought not to be rejected on the
narrow ground of States' rights. Attention has
previously been drawn (par 1.307) to absurd distinctions
with regard to compensation existing between the States.
The need for a national scheme was there stressed. If
the Woodhouse scheme is though to be defective, let us
devise a better one. Such a scheme can only be effective if enacted by the National Parliament. Uniform
legislation in all the States and Territories on the
initiative of the Standing Committee of Attorneys-
General - such as the Companies Acts and Hire-Purchase
Acts - has not remained uniform for long. Some
urgently needed uniform reforms which the States have
considered - such as reform of the Sale of Goods Acts
and of consumer credit law - have become enmeshed in
the wheels of the Standing Committee's machine and have
not emerged into the light of day. The chances of a
motorist being subject to a basically similar law if he
injures someone as he travels around Australia are slim
indeed unless the Federal Parliament is given power to
act, if need be by a reference on the part of all the
States under section 51(xxxvii) of the Constitution.
The financing of an adequate scheme of compensation and
rehabilitation can only come from the Federal purse.

6.103 Nevertheless, it would be open to any injured
person who believed that he could do better at common
law or under a State statute, to ask the High Court to
declare invalid at least that provision of the Act
which declares that an action does not lie in respect
of damages where a benefit is payable in respect of the
incapacity suffered, whether or not a claim for the

benefit has been lodged (s 97). Thus we shall glance
briefly at the possible constitutional powers under
which the scheme could be supported.

  6.104 Insurance. It is unlikely that the scheme as
a whole could be supported by section 51(xiv) of the
Constitution, which gives the Parliament power to make
laws with respect to insurance. Although the view was
apparently expressed confidently at one time that a
social security law could be justified as a law with
respect to insurance,[2] it seems to be generally
accepted today that this is not so.[3] While the payment
of benefits under the scheme depends on a contingent,
uncertain event, as does insurance, there is nothing
equivalent to the payment of premiums, which must
surely be regarded as an essential element of
insurance.[4] Instead the Parliament will almost
certainly rely on its taxing powers (Constitution,
s 51(ii)) to raise the funds out of which it will from
time to time appropriate moneys for the payment of
benefits (s 119; see Sec 2).

  6.105 Section 99 probably depends for its validity
on the insurance power. This section, if valid, would
override State legislation (Constitution, s 109) and
prevent the States exercising compulsion on anyone to
insure in respect of personal injury or death. Thus
the compulsory third party motor vehicle insurance

---

2.   See G Sawer, _Australian Federal Politics and Law_,
     _1929-49_ (1963), 120.
3.   The foundation of the view against social security
     being a form of insurance seems to have been a
     note by M E L Cantor, "National Insurance in its
     Constitutional Aspects" (1928) 2 ALJ 219.
4.   For a recent case on the meaning of "insurance" in
     a non-constitutional context, see _Department of_
     Trade and Industry v _St Christopher's Motorists'_
     Association Ltd [1974] 1 All ER 395.

schemes and compulsory employers' liability and workers'
compensation insurance schemes would fall to the ground.
In particular the section would deprive the States of
the right to require insurance against personal injury
or death as a condition of registration of a motor
vehicle (s 99(2)). Whether such a provision, which
creates the situation that a person need <u>not</u> insure, is
a law with respect to insurance or incidental thereto
(Constitution, s 51(xiv) and (xxxix)) may only be
determined if a State were to continue in force its
compulsory insurance legislation and try to enforce it.
The challenge would then be to the State legislation by
someone whose interest it would be to show that section
99 of the National Compensation Act was valid. On the
other hand the States may themselves seek to take the
initiative in having their own laws declared binding.
In any event the matter being one "as to the limits
inter se of the Constitutional powers of the Commonwealth and of those of any State or States"
(Constitution, s 74) will have to be finally determined
by the High Court of Australia.

   6.106 <u>Invalid Pensions</u>. The payment of weekly
benefits for total and partial incapacity, whether as a
result of injury or sickness, can undoubtedly be
supported under placitum (xxiii) of section 51 of the
Constitution, "Invalid and old-age pensions". However,
this head of power would not cover lump-sum payments
for disfigurement (Chap 4, Sec 4) and expenses and
losses (Chap 4, Sec 5). Nor would it cover the
pensions and other benefits payable on death (Chap 4,
Sec 6).

6.107 <u>Social Services Power</u>. Most, if not all, the
benefits which cannot be classified as "invalid
pensions" would probably be within the powers conferred
by placitum (xxiiiA) of section 51, inserted into the
Constitution by referendum in 1946. This expressly
provides for the provision of "widows' pensions". It
also allows for the provision of "sickness ...
benefits". In what is its only real expression of
opinion on Constitutional matters, the committee states
that "'injury' conditions are actually embraced by and
<u>included within</u> the meaning of the word 'sickness'"
(<u>Report</u>, Vol 1, par 225, emphasis in original). Since
the word "benefits", as opposed to "pensions", is here
used, lump-sum payments are presumably authorized (cf
Dixon J in <u>British Medical Association</u> v <u>Commonwealth</u>
(1949) 79 CLR 201, 259-60). The Act does not purport
to "authorize any form of civil conscription" and thus
there should be no difficulty with that limit which the
placitum places on Parliament's power, however far the
limit extends.[5] Funeral benefits (par 4.601) and the
lump-sum payments to widows (par 4.604) alone do not
find a ready place in placitum (xxiiiA); perhaps they
could be treated as "family allowances".

6.108 <u>Inconsistency</u>. In section 97(1) the intention
of the Parliament is expressed to be "that a benefit in
respect of incapacity or death as the result of
personal injury or sickness is to be in substitution
for any damages recoverable or payable in respect of
that injury, sickness or death, whatever the cause of
action or basis of liability and whether the cause of
action is actionable at the suit of, or the liability
is enforceable by, the incapacitated person or some

---

5. See the different opinions on this issue contained
    in the <u>British Medical Association</u> case, <u>supra</u>.

other person". Subsection (2) prevents this intention
from being circumvented by failure to lodge a claim for
benefit. Then subsection (3) provides that an "action
or other proceeding does not lie in respect of damages
to which this section applies". "Damages" includes
(a) compensation and (b) payment under a compromise or
settlement of a claim for damages (s 4(1)). In this
way the Act tries to "cover the field" of payment for
injuries and sickness giving rise to claims for benefit.
If it does so successfully, section 109 of the
Constitution will operate to make inconsistent State
law invalid. However, it seems that, despite the
expressed intention it would have to be shown that the
prohibition on the co-existence of common law and State
remedies was "incidental" (Constitution, s 51(xxxix))
to the powers utilized in the payment of benefits.
This appears to be in Constitutional terms the most
vulnerable part of the whole scheme. Indeed, should it
ultimately be held by the High Court that the abolition
of existing remedies is not incidental to the powers
conferred by the Constitution, it may be impossible to
sever it from the rest of the Act, and maintain the
payment of benefits, for the very reason that the
Parliament has expressed its intention that those
benefits are to be in substitution for the existing
remedies.

6.109 If the abolition of existing remedies is
within the Constitutional power of the Federal
Parliament, no difficulty should arise with the requirement (under s 98) that a person who succeeds in
recovering damages (in Australia or elsewhere) must pay
to Australia a sum up to the amount of the damages
received. However, if section 97 is _ultra vires_, then
section 98, in so far as it does require repayment of

the damages (see par 3.102), must surely fall too. On
the other hand, if section 97 is ultra vires, but can
be severed from the rest of the Act, section 98 may
survive on an interpretation that all it requires is a
repayment of any benefits received (see par 3.102),
which would seem to be clearly "incidental" to the
actual payment of the benefits.

Sec 2:   COST AND FINANCING

6.201   The committee arrived at estimates of the cost
of the different parts of the scheme relating to injury,
congenital disability and sickness on the basis of what
it would have cost in 1973-4 if the scheme had already
been operating for many years. During the phasing-in
period of the scheme, and even for some years thereafter, the actual costs in 1973-4 money values will, of
course, be less because people incapacitated before the
various commencing dates (see par 3.205) will be
ineligible for a time, or altogether (if they have
already recovered damages). The statistical team
assisting the committee had recourse to Australian
statistics, where available, and to those of some overseas countries. Full details are set out in Part 9 of
the Compendium. As previously mentioned the committee
said that it was "able to say with confidence that to
the extent that there may be errors they certainly do
not lie on the side of under-estimation of the costs of
the proposals" (Report, Vol 1, par 491). However, no
cost figures are available as a result of the extension
of payments for total incapacity to the first week for
persons injured in circumstances where workers'
compensation is now payable (par 4.208) and the
inclusion of benefits for minor permanent partial

incapacities (par 4.306). Other amendments to the
committee's proposals may also increase the cost of the
scheme as a whole.

6.202 Cost of Injury Scheme. On the basis of the
committee's proposals the net cost of the injury scheme,
excluding hospital, medical and other expenses (see
Chap 4, Sec 5), would, if a "plateau" had been reached
in 1973-4, have been $325 million. To include
congenital disabilities, as the committee recommended
(see par 3.202), would add $130 million to the cost.
The sickness part of the scheme would add another
$1,200 million. The total cost of the combined scheme
would thus be $1,655 million. A break-up of these
figures is conveniently set out in Table XII of Volume
1 of the Report; fuller statistical calculations are in
Part 9 of the Compendium.

6.203 Comparison with Present Systems. As compared
with the $325 million estimated cost of the injury
scheme in full operation in 1973-4, the actual premiums
collected in Australia in 1972-3, including costs of
self-insurers, for employers' liability and compulsory
motor vehicle insurance was $510 million. Updating
that figure to 1973-4 produced an estimate of premiums
collected, including costs of self-insurers, of $665
million. Since the scheme's estimated cost excluded
hospital and medical expenses, which are included in
the present systems, $95 million has to be deducted
from the figure of $665 million. Thus the National
Compensation Scheme in respect of injuries would cost
only $325 million as against $570 million, the actual
cost of the existing systems, a saving of $245 million
in one year. There would be other savings as a result
of it being unnecessary to pay some social security
benefits now payable to injured people who fail to

recover compensation at common law or under workers'
compensation. (The above figures all appear in Table
XI of Vol 1 of the Report.)

6.204 Moreover, the actual premiums collected under
the existing systems in 1973-4 were almost certainly
too low to provide adequate funds for the benefits to
be paid in the future. Recent huge increases in
compulsory third party premiums in Victoria, for
instance, are some recognition of this fact. On an
"over-conservative" basis, the committee estimated the
cost of adequate premiums (allowing for inflation at
less than 9 to 10 per cent) in 1973-4 at $845 million
(Report, Vol 1, pars 476-9). Deducting $95 million for
hospital and medical expenses, one arrives at a figure
of $750 million, which is the truly comparable figure
with the scheme's $325 million per year for injury.
Most of this huge saving to the community would come
from cutting down on the expensive administrative costs
of the present systems (see pars 1.318-20), but some
would result from money no longer being squandered on
generous settlements for "pain and suffering" in
comparatively trivial cases. Yet the scheme ensures
that all people who really need it are more adequately
compensated than under the various existing systems.
Further savings, not taken account of in the comparison
between $325 million and $750 million, would result
from a lessened need for social security benefits and
for the time of judges, jurymen and court officials.

6.205 Effect on Legal Profession. Although the
community as a whole would benefit from all these
savings, there are certain costs which would affect
particular groups, especially the legal profession and
the insurance industry. Some lawyers derive a substantial part of their income from claims for damages and
workers' compensation, whether they act generally for

claimants or insurers. Most lawyers probably make some
money each year out of the present systems. Although
legal representation at departmental hearings and
appeals is permitted (pars 5.112 and 5.203), the
emphasis on freedom from dispute and adversary proceedings (except on an appeal to the court) will probably
lead to the employment of comparatively few lawyers.
The Report (Vol 1, par 163) quotes from No Fault on the
Roads, a recent publication of JUSTICE, the British
section of the International Commission of Jurists,
which stated that the committee which drew up the
proposals for a no-fault motor accident scheme for
Britain "was convinced that there is plenty of other
work for lawyers to do which would compensate for the
loss of work in the personal injuries field". In this
connexion, one might draw attention to the increased
availability of legal aid, which has put legal assistance within the reach of many members of the community
hitherto excluded. New fields are also opening for
lawyers as a result of legislation such as that dealing
with restrictive trade practices and prices justification, as a result of the proposed legislation on human
rights and civil liberties, and as a result of the
greater interest in consumer affairs and environment
protection. Adjustment should not be difficult for a
profession which claims to be learned.

6.206 Effect on Insurance Industry. The insurance
industry is likely to be more drastically affected. An
estimate by two representatives of the industry (Report,
Vol 1, Appendix 7, par 4) considered that the "market
as a whole will lose about 35 per cent of its income"
and that some individual insurers, particularly
Australian companies, would lose a much greater proportion. However, it must be recognized that it has been
repeatedly claimed by the industry that compulsory

third party and workers' compensation are the least
profitable areas of insurance. In the former, premiums
are rigidly controlled by State governments and are
often wholly inadequate to provide funds for rapidly
escalating damages awards. In recent years there has
been a wholesale exodus from this field by all but a
few insurers. Workers' compensation reserves have
suffered as a result of the tendency of State governments to increase benefits retrospectively. Thus in the
long run, the inability of the insurance industry to
cope with the problem of inflation would in any event
lead it rationally to decline to take on this type of
business. Personal accident insurance is probably not
widespread enough to cause the insurance industry
concern at its loss and there may in fact be more such
insurance by people who wish to cover themselves for
more than they could obtain under the Act. The effect
on life assurance is problematical; that type of
insurance is likely to be more significantly affected
by proposals for national superannuation.

   6.207 Nevertheless, in the short run the insurance
industry could be hard hit as it finds that it no
longer has any current premiums from which to make up
the deficiencies in its accumulated reserves. Disposal
of assets in those reserves would also further depress
stock-markets, which by 1976 might not have recovered
from their present low points. The committee had
difficulty in making recommendations to overcome these
difficulties because the industry as a whole failed to
provide it with the necessary information (Report, Vol
1, par 507). It believed that the problems could be
solved by discussions between the industry and the
Government during the period before the actual operation
of the scheme. Two representatives of the industry
suggested that the Government might offer to assume all

outstanding liabilities from any insurer which elected
to hand over its reserves (Report, Vol 1, Appendix 7,
par 9.6). Spokesmen for the Government have since
indicated their willingness to discuss all relevant
questions with the industry so as to arrive at a suitable accommodation. The matter of redundancy of staff
has, it is believed, already been given consideration.

6.208 Cost of Congenital Incapacity. To include
congenital incapacity within the National Compensation
Scheme would, on the committee's estimates, cost $130
million on 1973-4 figures (Report, Vol 1, Table XII.
There is a small discrepancy between the figure of $125
million payable as benefits for permanent, total,
congenital incapacity in this Table and $126 million,
the estimate appearing in the Compendium, Part 9, par
71. This is presumably due to rounding to the nearest
multiple of 5; rounding of other figures has been
upwards, eg, Compendium, Part 9, par 36.) Since the
combined cost of the scheme for injuries and congenital
disabilities would be only $455 million - still well
below the $570 million actual cost (and $750 million
"adequate" premium cost) of the existing systems - and
since it is difficult to distinguish between injuries
and other disabilities suffered before birth, the
committee recommended the immediate inclusion of
congenital incapacities within the scheme (see par
3.202).

6.209 Total Cost, Including Sickness. The estimated
cost of the sickness part of the scheme, on 1973-4
figures, is $1,200 million. Combined with the cost of
the injury scheme, including congenital disability, of
$455 million, the total cost would be $1,655 million.
Against this has to be offset a saving in social
security costs of $370 million (Report, Vol 1, par 471;
details are in the Compendium, Part 9, pars 102-9), and

the saving of the premiums for the existing systems of
compensation for injuries ($570 million "actual" or
$750 million "adequate": see par 6.204). Thus funds
for the whole comprehensive scheme would cost the
Australian community $715 million per year more than
the cost of the funds for the present piecemeal arrangements and only $535 million more than the funds for
those piecemeal arrangements should properly be costing.

6.210 Sources of Funds. The Act provides merely for
the appropriation of funds from time to time by the
Parliament (s 119). The committee recommended two new
taxes to replace current workers' compensation premiums
and compulsory third party motor vehicle insurance
premiums. The one tax would be a flat rate levy on
employers of 2 per cent of their bill for wages and
salaries (Report, Vol 1, par 498). The same levy would
apply to the income of self-employed people, who would
be entitled, like employers, to treat it as a deduction
from their assessable income for the purposes of income
tax (ibid, par 499). In both instances, it would not
be levied against earnings in excess of $26,000 per
annum, since that is the maximum on which earnings-
related compensation for total incapacity may be based
at the inception of the scheme (s 31; pars 4.210 and
4.214). The other new tax would be an excise tax of
10c a gallon on petrol and diesel oil. On 1973-4
figures these taxes would raise $600 million and $290
million respectively (Compendium, Part 9, pars 110-4).
This would be more than would be needed if the inuury
scheme alone were introduced. It might even be enough
during the early stages of the combined injury and
sickness scheme until the full costs of the "plateau"
stage were reached. In any event, the committee
recommended that any shortfall, either initially or
once the full costs were incurred, should be made up

from general taxes, from which social security is
presently financed (Report, Vol 1, par 505).

6.211   The Government has not decided whether to
accept the committee's recommendations as to the
methods of financing the scheme.   The whole question is
under study by the Treasury.   The 2 per cent levy on
wages and salaries is less than the average now paid by
industry in workers' compensation premiums.   However,
while some hazardous industries would benefit considerably, other industries would have to pay more than at
present.   The economic effects of a reduction in the
expenses of mining and manufacturing industries and the
increased costs of service industries need careful
study; they might well be beneficial at the present
time.   Self-employed people would have to pay a levy to
which there is at present no comparable expenditure,
though some of them may be saved personal accident
insurance premiums.   In return, however, they would
obtain a security which many of them now lack.   The
ordinary motorist would benefit greatly: if he
travelled 10,000 miles per year, his fuel bill would be
increased by $50 or less per year (depending on whether
the petrol consumption of his vehicle was 20 mpg or
more), and he would be saved third party insurance
premiums well in excess of that sum.   But as a consumer
he might then find that the costs of many of the goods
he buys has risen to cover increased transport costs.
Overall, the 10c a gallon excise tax might prove to be
unacceptably inflationary.

6.212   Differential Rating.   The committee in effect
rejected the theory of general deterrence put forward
in recent years by Professor G Calabresi of Yale
University (see particularly The Costs of Accidents
(1970)).   Briefly, that theory is that if the costs of
accidents are attributed to appropriate activities,

market forces will lead to a reduction in those
activities which are more hazardous, with a consequent
overall fall in the level of accidents. (This theory,
as Calabresi recognizes, needs to be qualified to
prevent hardship to people who are not able to distribute losses. Calabresi would also supplement it with
"specific deterrence".) The committee thought that
market conditions in Australia are not sufficiently
free to have the desired effect (Report, Vol 2, par
362). Undoubtedly, there are many other factors which
make up the price of particular goods and services
which would have a much more significant impact than
increased or reduced contributions towards the National
Compensation Scheme. There is also the difficulty of
identifying which of the many activities "responsible"
for an accident is the one on which the costs should
initially be placed.[1]

6.213 In any event, the committee regarded the 459
classifications of workers' compensation premiums in
New South Wales as "a sterile and cumbersome exercise"
(Report, Vol 1, par 496). It also found that North
American experience "suggests that merit rating can
even have an adverse effect on safety" (Report, Vol 2,
par 366). It considered the Ontario policy of penalty
ratings (ibid, pars 367-8) but concluded (ibid, par 369)
that any decision on such matters should await the
statistical data which will be available to the
National Safety Office once the scheme has been in
operation for some time. Meanwhile, incentives towards
safety must come from educating individual employers to

1.   See the exposition and criticism of the theory in
     P S Atiyah, Accidents, Compensation and the Law
     (1970), Chap 24. For a summary see Professor
     Atiyah's review of Calabresi's book in (1970) 44
     ALJ 297.

recognize that the loss of production and general
disruption due to accidents is a cost that can easily
be saved by adopting safety measures. Such costs are
likely to be much greater than any conceivable increase
in insurance premiums or their equivalent. A fact not
mentioned by the committee is that where premiums
increase with adverse workers' compensation experience,
employers are reluctant to engage workers whom they
regard as more susceptible to injury. This leads to
undesirable discriminatory employment practices and
often prevents the rehabilitation of partially disabled
workers.

Sec 3:   PROPOSALS CONCERNING REHABILITATION

6.301   "Rehabilitation" connotes the restoration of a
person to a previously held position, or the restoration
to a person of faculties he once possessed. The
proposals which the committee made go beyond this.
Volume 2, Part 2, of the Report starts with a quotation
from John Galsworthy: "A niche of usefulness and self-
respect exists for every man, however handicapped; but
that niche must be found for him." The committee's
proposals will help to find "that niche" for all the
handicapped members of our society; they are not aimed
merely at restoring the injured and sick to positions
they once held, but are also concerned to enable the
congenitally handicapped to fit as far as possible into
society and to realize their full potential there.
Hitherto, the committee maintains, society has paid far
too little attention to the needs of the handicapped
(Report, Vol 2, par 29). The solution proposed is to
provide comprehensively for social, vocational and
educational services, as well as medical services

(ibid, par 33). In place of the present inadequate and
fragmented facilities, the committee recommends a
centrally controlled, co-ordinated and comprehensive
plan. The central control is to come from a Rehabilitation Division of the proposed Social Welfare Policy
and Planning Department of the Australian Government,
but the administration is to be on a regional basis,
with funds made available to State Governments and
voluntary organizations (ibid, par 57).

   6.302 The committee sees the establishment of this
Rehabilitation Division as the first task in the
implementation of the National Rehabilitation Scheme
(ibid, par 58). Unlike the National Compensation
Scheme, which the committee devised in great detail and
for which it provided a blueprint in the draft Bill,
the details of the National Rehabilitation Scheme are
left to be worked out by the Rehabilitation Division
once it is established. The committee (ibid, par 59)
offers advice to the Division as to the order of
priority in which it should set about implementing the
Rehabilitation Scheme, making it clear that some
matters are only long-term objectives. The recommendations on all the specific points are, therefore, no
more than guidelines for the actual administrators.

   6.303 In these circumstances little more will be
attempted here than to reiterate the summary provided
by the committee of its own recommendations (Report,
Vol 2, pars 1 to 28; see also Vol 1, pars 447-67). As
already mentioned, the scheme should be administered on
a regional basis under the central control of the
Rehabilitation Division. In addition to a Regional
Director, each region should have an advisory committee
representing Government, local government and interested citizens and groups. Within each region there
should be at least (a) medical rehabilitation units and

a limited number of specialist medical rehabilitation
units; (b) mobile rehabilitation clinic teams; (c)
general rehabilitation centres; (d) sheltered workshops
and day activity centres; (e) accommodation and domiciliary services for handicapped persons; and (f) special
facilities for pre-school training and education of
handicapped children and for their accommodation.
Nationally, there should be provision for selective
placement of the disabled; aids, appliances and equipment should be made available free of charge to
handicapped people; assistance should be given with
regard to transport; architectural barriers should be
removed; staff for rehabilitation work should be
properly trained; research into rehabilitation should
be undertaken; and close liaison should be established
between the officials concerned with compensation and
those concerned with rehabilitation. The committee
also makes recommendations with regard to special
facilities required for particular groups, viz the
aged, mentally handicapped persons, blind persons and
autistic persons. In the following paragraphs some of
these points are expanded by reference to what is said
in the body of Volume 2 of the Report.

6.304 Staff Training. Top priority, in the
committee's view, should be given to ensuring substantially increased training facilities for the staff for
the medical rehabilitation units and the general
rehabilitation centres. This is dealt with in Volume 2,
Part 8. Medical schools should become more conscious
of rehabilitation so as to instil in young doctors an
awareness of the need to treat the whole man. Chairs
of Physical and Rehabilitation Medicine should be
established. Para-medical staff, in particular
rehabilitation counsellors, should be trained in

increased numbers. The highly skilled nature of the
work of therapists should be recognized and adequately
rewarded; therapists should be represented at senior
management level and should participate fully in
planning; their status generally should be upgraded.
There is need, too, to encourage more clinical psych-
ologists.

6.305 <u>Medical Rehabilitation Services</u>. The second
priority, according to the committee, should be the
provision of substantial funds to assist the States in
the establishment of full medical rehabilitation
services, particularly in rural areas (Vol 2, pars
77-95). There should be medical rehabilitation units
associated with the 42 major metropolitan hospitals in
State capitals. In addition, Appendix 2 sets out a
list of some 80 non-metropolitan hospitals to which it
is suggested medical rehabilitation units be attached.
These basic units would provide, under medical
direction, physiotherapy, occupational and speech
therapy, social worker services and rehabilitation
counselling and domiciliary services. They "should be
divorced as far as possible from the hospital
atmosphere" and, where practicable, "should be within a
reasonable distance of general rehabilitation centres".
Mobile rehabilitation clinic teams, comprising a
rehabilitation medical officer, rehabilitation
counsellor, social worker, nursing sister and therapist,
should visit towns and smaller centres where rehabilitation units have not been established. Furthermore,
there should be a few specialist medical rehabilitation
units, such as for quadriplegics and paraplegics.
These would almost certainly be attached to one of the
major teaching hospitals in the capital cities. "They
would provide a full range of sophisticated equipment

and facilities and offer advanced medical and para-
medical treatment required for special post-acute
management and long-term medical rehabilitation
assistance in the case of particular types of severe
disability."

6.306 General Rehabilitation Centres. Next in
priority comes the establishment of general rehabilitation centres (Vol 2, pars 96-116), so that ultimately
there should be 16 of these in metropolitan areas and
another 16 in rural districts. Again, the more
immediate need is in the rural districts. The function
of these centres is to enable persons with severe
residual disabilities to be fitted for employment,
whether full-time, part-time or sheltered; or to resume
a former role as housewife; or to become capable of an
independent or semi-independent life at home or in
appropriate self-contained residential accommodation.
Here would be available services for assessment,
guidance, counselling, training and work preparation
and placement, which make up vocational rehabilitation.
The centres would be more comprehensive than the
rehabilitation centres now conducted by the Department
of Social Security, which have achieved some notable
successes. There would be close liaison with the
medical rehabilitation units; but job placement and
finding suitable living accommodation would be the
concern of the general rehabilitation centres, rather
than of the medical units.

6.307 Aids to Living. Reference has already been
made (par 4.505) to some of the committee's recommendations for the provision and maintenance of artificial
limbs, appliances and equipment (Vol 2, pars 157-86).
The committee (ibid, pars 187-9) also wishes to see an
expansion of domiciliary services, such as home-nursing,
housekeeping, sitters, meals-on-wheels, social work and

occupational therapy. In extreme cases full-time
personal attendants should be provided without cost to
the person in need. Transport costs to and from
rehabilitation centres should be met by the Government;
such centres should also have flexible hours in their
out-patient departments to enable handicapped people to
be transported by relatives and friends (ibid, pars
191-3). Transport of the disabled to and from work
should be borne in mind in the design of public transport facilities (ibid, par 195). Assistance should be
given in the purchase of specially adapted motor
vehicles; in the training of handicapped drivers to use
them; and in providing special parking facilities
(ibid, pars 194 and 196-9). Governments in Australia
should follow the lead of the United States in legislating for an architectural barrier-free environment and
should set an example by making necessary adaptations
to their existing buildings. A public relations
campaign should be conducted to make people more aware
of the problem of barriers to the handicapped (ibid,
pars 200-5). Recreational facilities should also be
provided for the handicapped (ibid, pars 206-9).
Finally, research should be undertaken into improving
the various aids to living that could be made available
to the handicapped (ibid, pars 231-7).

   6.308 Compensation and Rehabilitation. The committee
recommends that compensation benefits should continue
to be paid throughout the period of rehabilitation,
including any period of training (Vol 2, par 284).
However, close liaison must be maintained between the
Compensation Department and the Rehabilitation Division
to minimize abuse and to ensure the earliest possible
return to useful activity of those who are receiving
compensation (Vol 1, par 468). Compensation officials
must refer beneficiaries promptly to rehabilitation

personnel if the rehabilitative aims of the scheme as a
whole are to be achieved (ibid, par 469) and if charges
that it is a charter for malingerers are to be avoided.
Many people now regarded as malingerers would undoubtedly return to work if they had the support and
assistance of social workers and vocational counsellors.
If such services are made available, it will only be in
the rare case that the Secretary will need to exercise
his power under section 117(c) of the Act to suspend,
postpone or cancel payment of a benefit to an
incapacitated person who refuses or fails to take
action that the Secretary considers it reasonable for
him to take in order to terminate, or to reduce the
extent of, his incapacity.

Sec 4:   PROPOSALS CONCERNING SAFETY

6.401   If accidents are prevented, compensation and
rehabilitation are unnecessary. The committee found
that too little has been and is being done in Australia
to prevent accidents. Not enough is known about the
real causes of accidents: on the one hand, there is a
too-ready attribution of responsibility to individual
blameworthiness; on the other, there is a fatalistic
acceptance of the inevitability of accidents. While
some organizations, such as the voluntary National
Safety Council of Australia, have done valuable work,
much of the effort being made in Australia to eliminate
or reduce accidents is fragmented and lacks central
co-ordination. Furthermore, attempts to create a safe
environment are hampered by inadequate statistics of
injury - particularly in the home and at places of
recreation - and consequent ignorance of the true
circumstances in which accidents occur.

6.402 National Safety Office. Thus the main
recommendation of the committee is the establishment of
a National Safety Office to "provide money, resources,
expertise and direction"; to maintain proper statistics;
and to stimulate scientific research (Report, Vol 2,
pars 297-8, 308 and 311). It would also systematically
evaluate safety education programmes (ibid, par 313)
and establish safety display centres (ibid, par 315).
Further, it would investigate methods of implementing
suggestions which the committee makes with regard to
the training of children and adults in matters of
safety (ibid, pars 316-21).

6.403 Legislation. The committee is of the opinion
that the mass and prolixity of laws, particularly with
regard to industrial safety and road traffic, may have
reached the point where specific prohibitions become
counter-productive (ibid, par 300). "A determined
effort should be made to revise, harmonize and up-date
the large body of existing laws on safety. It is
desirable ... that the style should be simplified and
the number of relevant statutes reduced. Uniformity in
Federal and State law is a high priority" (ibid, par
302). The National Safety Office should seek to
achieve this aim and administration of the hopefully
consolidated and simplified legislation "should not
proliferate among different Departments" (ibid). No
guidance is offered as to how these admirable objectives are to overcome inter-State and State-Federal
jealousies.

6.404 Product Safety. In one area the committee
thought existing legislation insufficient. It was of
the opinion that consumer protection laws, where they
occurred at State-level, laid down inadequate penalties
for breach of safety standards; nor were the regulation-
making powers under these laws used frequently enough

(<u>ibid</u>, par 331). It remains to be seen whether these
particular deficiencies will be remedied now that the
Australian Government has entered the field with
sections 62 and 63 of the Trade Practices Act 1974.
However, the committee wishes the Parliament to go
further and enact a Consumer Product Safety Act,
similar to that enacted by the United States Congress,
which would confer power, <u>inter alia</u>, to order recall,
repair, replacement or provision of a refund where a
product proved to be defective or dangerous (<u>ibid</u>, pars
329 and 332). The National Safety Office would not
only administer the Act (<u>ibid</u>, par 332(h)), but would
take action to reduce the frequency and severity of
injuries involving consumer products by adopting
programmes such as the National Electronic Injuries
Surveillance System established by the United States
Bureau of Product Safety (<u>ibid</u>, pars 324-8).

6.405 <u>Occupational Safety</u>. The committee adduces
evidence showing a dramatic fall in the frequency rate
of injuries experienced by Australian companies and
organizations after the introduction of proper safety
programmes (<u>ibid</u>, Appendix 5). Such programmes need to
be "sold" to employers (<u>ibid</u>, par 355(m)), who must be
convinced of the disruption to their production which
each accident causes. Companies should be required to
include information about accidents and preventive
measures in their annual reports (<u>ibid</u>, par 341).
Employees must be encouraged to participate with
employers in safety programmes (<u>ibid</u>, pars 345-7).
Training of safety personnel should be extended (<u>ibid</u>,
pars 348-53). Although sharing the reluctance of the
Robens <u>Report on Safety and Health at Work</u> (1972) in
England to rely exclusively on legislating for safety,
the committee nevertheless recommends the adoption of
the United States Occupational Safety and Health Act

1970 (ibid, par 344). Among other things, this "Act
gives employee representatives the important privileges
of the right to accompany an OSHA inspector on his
factory tour of inspection and to confer with him
privately about any work hazards. Employees may also
file complaints and are expressly protected from being
dismissed or from any reprisal for initiating such
complaints. They are additionally entitled to request
inspections if they believe their working conditions
violate standards" (ibid, Appendix 6).

    6.406 Road Safety. Although the committee recognizes
continuing serious deficiencies in the Australian
approach to the problem of road safety, the Report
contains no specific proposals in this area, beyond
urging that the recommended National Safety Office
maintain a close liaison with the National Office of
Road Safety (shortly to be established by the Australian
Government) and co-operate with other road safety
organizations to produce a co-ordinated effort. The
reason for this reticence is the recommendation by the
Expert Group on Road Safety, set up by the Department
of Shipping and Transport, under the chairmanship of
Mr Justice Meares, that there be established a National
Office of Road Safety. Specific recommendations can be
expected to be forthcoming from that body.

    6.407 Economic Incentives. As already mentioned
(pars 6.212-3) the committee rejected the idea that the
method of raising funds for the National Compensation
Scheme should be used to provide economic incentives
towards safety (Report, Vol 2, pars 359-69). It
preferred a uniform, flat-rate levy on all employers
and self-employed people to replace existing differential workers' compensation premiums. It also
rejected the notion of merit ratings, ie reduction of
premiums for good accident records, since this can lead

to the withholding of reports of accidents and the
contesting of claims for compensation (<u>ibid</u>, par 366).
The question of penalty rating should, in the
committee's opinion, await the collection of statistics
by the National Safety Office. Such new data will also
allow the introduction of possible fresh approaches,
based on solid research (<u>ibid</u>, par 369).

INDEX

CHILDREN

COMMITTEE OF INQUIRY see WOODHOUSE COMMITTEE

COMMON LAW see also EXISTING SCHEMES

CONGENITAL INCAPACITY

CONSTITUTIONAL VALIDITY   6.101-9

COSTS

CRIMINALS   3.404

DEATH BENEFITS see also CHILDREN, FUNERAL EXPENSES, WIDOWS' BENEFITS

DE FACTO WIVES   4.603, 4.607, 4.615

DISFIGUREMENT   4.101, 4.401-5